inside magazines

inside magazines

independentpopculturemagazines

Edited by Patrik Andersson & Judith Steedman

Thames & Hudson

First published in the
United Kingdom in 2002
by Thames & Hudson Ltd,
181A High Holborn,
London WC1V 7QX

© 2002 Patrik Andersson and
Judith Steedman / BIS Publishers
The copyright on the individual
texts and designs is held by the
respective authors and designers.

British Library Cataloguing-
in-Publication Data
A catalogue record for this book is
available from the British Library

ISBN 0-500-28364-8

Printed and bound
in Singapore

Contents

6 Preface
Joseph Monteyne

8 Introduction
Patrik Andersson and Judith Steedman

14 Beyond Magazines
Patrik Andersson

21 A Select Survey of Independent Pop Culture Magazines

120 Close to You
Jeff Rian

130 Vancouver Soundscape Project
Robin Mitchell

134 Glamour Part One: People
Pipel: Maria Ben Saad, Stefania Malmsten and Tina Axelsson

144 *Petit Glam*
Co Ito and Takaya Goto

154 Present, Past and Future: A Personal Quest
Uscha Pohl

166 Four Proposals for Living Units
Ian Skedd

172 Special Edit.
Ref.

184 Prototype for New Understanding
Brian Jungen

188 *Sec. 09*
Sec.

198 Welcome to *Asianpunkboy* World
Terence Koh

202 A Really Difficult Text About *Re- Magazine* by a 12 Year Old Girl
Re- Magazine

210 L.A. Independent
Casey McKinney

222 Jesus vs. Satan, and Briefs
Raif Adelberg

228 Interviews
Re-, Purple, Index, Made in USA, Butt

234 Moments in the Life of the Artist
Myfanwy MacLeod

Preface

Joseph Monteyne

One could begin a discussion of the magazine with new forms of print that contributed to the years of civil war and ultimately regicide in 17th-century England. Ephemeral tracts, serial news sheets and broadsides had an incredibly powerful effect on the organization of political groups and also served to bring together the communities of taste soon formed around the nexus of Restoration London's coffee houses. However, it seems more germane for the contents of this book to begin at the end of the 1960s, when, under the influence of the ideas of Marshall McLuhan, many writers pondered the fate of the serial publication. By this time the era of the printed word, according to McLuhan, had ceded to forms of electronic communication. James Ford, in *Magazines for Millions* (1969), predicted that in the very near future we would roll out of bed and turn a knob on an "Instant-Fac" in order to begin a printout of a *Morning Magazine*, the contents of which would be pre-ordered and personalized. This *Morning Magazine* would be designed for the now "less-perfect human eye" not used to reading, and would even include three-dimensional effects with tactile and olfactory supplements. A few years later Roland Wolsley, in *The Changing Magazine* (1973), forecast that by

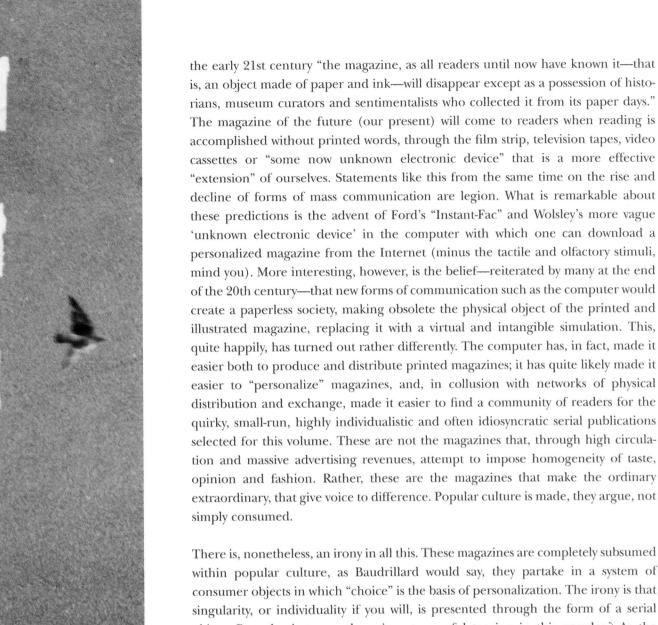

the early 21st century "the magazine, as all readers until now have known it—that is, an object made of paper and ink—will disappear except as a possession of historians, museum curators and sentimentalists who collected it from its paper days." The magazine of the future (our present) will come to readers when reading is accomplished without printed words, through the film strip, television tapes, video cassettes or "some now unknown electronic device" that is a more effective "extension" of ourselves. Statements like this from the same time on the rise and decline of forms of mass communication are legion. What is remarkable about these predictions is the advent of Ford's "Instant-Fac" and Wolsley's more vague 'unknown electronic device' in the computer with which one can download a personalized magazine from the Internet (minus the tactile and olfactory stimuli, mind you). More interesting, however, is the belief—reiterated by many at the end of the 20th century—that new forms of communication such as the computer would create a paperless society, making obsolete the physical object of the printed and illustrated magazine, replacing it with a virtual and intangible simulation. This, quite happily, has turned out rather differently. The computer has, in fact, made it easier both to produce and distribute printed magazines; it has quite likely made it easier to "personalize" magazines, and, in collusion with networks of physical distribution and exchange, made it easier to find a community of readers for the quirky, small-run, highly individualistic and often idiosyncratic serial publications selected for this volume. These are not the magazines that, through high circulation and massive advertising revenues, attempt to impose homogeneity of taste, opinion and fashion. Rather, these are the magazines that make the ordinary extraordinary, that give voice to difference. Popular culture is made, they argue, not simply consumed.

There is, nonetheless, an irony in all this. These magazines are completely subsumed within popular culture, as Baudrillard would say, they partake in a system of consumer objects in which "choice" is the basis of personalization. The irony is that singularity, or individuality if you will, is presented through the form of a serial object. But who is to say there is not a useful tension in this paradox? As the following pages will show, the distinctiveness of these publications emerges at the level of both subject and object. The subjects of the magazines are certainly unique—from the particular fashions of the fans of different bands to quite simply no subject at all—as are the physical objects of the magazines themselves. Of the two poles, it is the latter that cannot be duplicated by virtual forms of communication. The printed object has a sensuous aspect—it was there all the time—that would be lacking in electronic magazines: there is a tactility to the paper as it rolls across the thumb, you can smell the ink, the design has a weight, a body, it appeals to the senses as well as the intellect. Thus, it is ironic that these magazines often seem closer to the singularity of the art object than to the mass-produced serial object so characteristic of popular culture.

7

Introduction

Patrik Andersson & Judith Steedman

Inside Magazines is a visual record of a recently emerged publishing region located in-between the world of underground zines and that of mass-marketed magazines. As a select survey of independent pop culture magazines, this book reflects the hybrid nature of publications that create an intersection for art, music, fashion, design and youth culture. Treating this contemporary material, *Inside Magazines* serves as an archeology of style and design politics resulting from individual attempts to transform the public sphere of late capitalism into an image of their own. The idea of this survey is not to fix the individual ideas represented by each magazine but to set in motion a dialogue between them. This book is by no means meant to be a complete survey of this new publishing genre. Instead, *Inside Magazines* provides an inside view of a select number of publications that we feel have managed to push the limits set by the mainstream publishing industry.

As a survey, this book is both incomplete and at times incongruous. But its pseudo-archival structure reflects the process by which the material was gathered. A trip here, an email there: the most rewarding aspect of making this book has been the meetings we have had with the individuals who contributed their opinions and creative output. Our own editorial strategy has been to mimic the editorial approaches that attracted us to these particular magazines in the first place. To stay true to the idea of independent magazines, we gave some contributors a chance to intervene in our book with autonomous projects. This book is therefore not just a catalogue of magazines but a collection of historical essays, artist projects, mini-magazines and insightful interviews. It is meant to function just as well in an academic setting as it should in a living room, a magazine shop, a bookstore or a gallery.

ABOUT THE CONTRIBUTORS

Joseph Monteyne (London)

Joseph Monteyne is a postdoctoral fellow at the Courtauld Institute of Art and the Paul Mellon Centre for Studies in British Art in London. Monteyne's dissertation, *Space of Print and Printed Spaces in Restoration London: 1660-1685,* opens up an important discussion of the emergence of print culture and social space. Of particular interest to this book, Monteyne has theorized about the beginning of serial print (such as newspapers and magazines) and the advent of coffee houses. Monteyne has also published essays on contemporary popular culture and art in numerous magazines and journals.

Jeff Rian (Paris)

Jeff Rian is a writer and musician living in Paris. He is a professor of art history at École des Beaux Arts, Nîmes and Paris, and is associate editor of *Purple* magazine. Rian has published books and catalogues on subjects ranging from contemporary art and culture to the history of communication. His latest publication, *The Buckshot Lexicon* (2001), treats subjects as diverse as weeds and abstraction. For this book Rian has written a text about "anorexia and magazines, hiding in closets, purging, anxiety, wanting to be skinny and to be a singer, being creative and shy and a little rascal all at the same time."

Robin Mitchell (Vancouver)

Robin Mitchell is a freelance graphic designer who has worked most recently with Quattro Records, Japan; Rodney Graham for the Dia Center for the Arts, New York; and the House of Envy, Vancouver. She is co-creator and designer of the clothing label Salut les Poules. For *Inside Magazines* she has contributed excerpts from her independent book project *Vancouver Soundscapes.*

Maria Ben Saad, Stefania Malmsten, Tina Axelsson (Stockholm)

Maria Ben Saad was the fashion editor and Stefania Malmsten was the art director of Swedish fashion magazine *Bibel.* Since the magazine was closed down by its publisher in 2000 they have set up the fashion/media consultancy Pipel with the aim to pursue the ideas from *Bibel* within different media. For this book they have collaborated with cinematographer Tina Axelsson to produce a photo essay and interviews related to a short documentary film about glamour. The presentation "Glamour Part One: People" features stills from their film with a written commentary dealing with themes such as transformation, aspiration for glamour and fashion as a means of survival.

Petit Glam (Tokyo)

"Style, Culture, Fashion; Groovy Trends for Glamour People." *Petit Glam* is an extravagantly designed series of magazines, with each issue profiling a variety of international artists, book designers, fashion designers, industrial designers, dance troupes or photographers. For *Inside Magazines,* Co Ito and Takaya Goto have prepared 10 descriptive pages about films, books, publications, and a special art project, offering us a rare glimpse into the extraordinary object and resource that is *Petit Glam.*

Uscha Pohl (New York)

Former Vivienne Westwood style model and guest lecturer at the Royal College of Art, London, Uscha Pohl is an artist and designer who runs the fashion enterprise and art gallery Up&Co, from where she publishes her magazine *VERY* four times a year as well as the biannual *VERYstyleguide* to London and New York. *VERY* magazine is based on the concept of a curated group exhibition in a gallery. Artists working in different media and in different creative fields are featured quarterly. Uscha Pohl has contributed a playful history of magazines/art magazines that aims to position the current situation of independent magazine publishing.

Ian Skedd (Vancouver)

Ian Skedd is an artist who uses post-minimalist strategies to explore ways in which an individual negotiates private and public spaces through a relationship with systems of light and architecture. *Inside Magazines* has allotted five pages to serve as a catalogue for his recent exhibition at the Trylowsky Gallery in Vancouver, Canada. The work, *Living Units I-IV*, is based on the layout of his own downtown apartment. Through a process of repetition, these sculptures explore dichotomies between private and public domains by negotiating the inner and outer spaces of architecture.

Ref. (Tokyo)

Rather than being a mainstream magazine about music and fashion, the independent publication *Ref.* documents the fans of music and fashion. Publisher Yutaro Oka, editor Keiko Maeda and Synchro Design Tokyo have designed a 40 page special issue for *Inside Magazines*.

Brian Jungen (Vancouver)

Featured in this book, Brian Jungen's *Prototype for New Understanding* #5 and #6 put up an astute challenge to popular conceptions about identity as defined by traditional ethnography, art and fashion. By re-configuring the aesthetic traditions of avant-garde art and mass culture, Jungen sets in motion a dialectical play between his First Nations and Swiss background. Living in Vancouver, Canada, Jungen has exhibited internationally, most recently at KIASMA, Helsinki, and the Fruitmarket Gallery, Edinburgh. His work is also included in many private and public collections, including the National Gallery, Canada.

Sec. (Amsterdam)

This independently published magazine is focused on contemporary photography (made without commercial intent) that blurs the boundaries between art, fashion, design and the everyday. For this book, *Sec.* is launching its latest issue inside *Inside Magazines*. Designed by Roosje Klap, "sports" is the theme for this ninth issue.

Terence Koh (Vancouver/New York)

Terence Koh is an art director and illustrator living and working in Vancouver and New York City. He is editor and designer of *Asianpunkboy* magazine and has previously worked with the limited-edition art and fashion publication *Visionaire*. For *Inside Magazines*, Koh has produced an illustration and photo essay that gives insight into the world of *Asianpunkboy*.

Jop van Bennekom (Amsterdam)

Jop van Bennekom is a writer living and working in Amsterdam. He is editor-in-chief and designer of the Dutch independent publications *Butt* and *Re-* magazine. For this book, van Bennekom and his editorial team at *Re-* have contributed a series of interviews as well as a text that looks at *Re-* magazine from the "awkward," perspective of a 12 year-old girl named Astrid.

Casey McKinney (Los Angeles)

Casey McKinney is the editor and founder of a full-color, completely non-commercial art/literature magazine that has existed under titles as diverse as *Animal Stories* magazine, *Mall Punk* magazine, and *Ghost Stories* magazine. Each issue changes title, which is determined by a specific theme. In this way the magazine is killed off after each issue, ensuring a limited circulation and a broad range of flexible topics. For *Inside Magazines*, Casey has written and designed a "coverless mini-magazine" that discusses his own zine and influences in Los Angeles. This includes a discussion of magazines such as *Snowflake, American Homebody* and *Sad* magazine, and an interview with Raymond Pettibon.

Raif Adelberg (Vancouver)

Raif Adelberg is a graphic illustrator and artist working in Vancouver, Canada, where he runs Twentyfour, a clothing store and art gallery. For *Inside Magazines*, Adelberg has produced a "interactive" art works.

Myfanwy MacLeod (Vancouver)

Over the past few years, Myfanwy MacLeod has produced provocative images and objects which bridge humor and pop-culture psychology with the intellectual rigor and aesthetic attention associated with high art traditions. MacLeod exhibits internationally, including at the Melbourne Biennale, the Vancouver Art Gallery, Catriona Jeffries Gallery, Vancouver and the VTO Gallery, London. In February 2002, she has an exhibition "Comic Release: Negotiating Identity for a New Generation," at the Pittsburgh Centre for Contemporary Art. For *Inside Magazines*, MacLeod has produced four paintings which stage the problematics of art making.

Judith Steedman (Vancouver)

Designer and co-editor of *Inside Magazines*, Judith Steedman is the principal of Steedman Design, a graphic design studio in Vancouver, Canada. Specializing in art books, Steedman has designed books for artists and writers such as Francis Alys, Eija-Liisa Ahtila, Douglas Coupland, Stan Douglas, Ken Lum, Walter Marchetti and Bing Thom Architects. Steedman co-curated the exhibition *Supersonic Transport: A Survey of Independent Pop Culture Magazines*. She holds degrees in English literature and graphic design from the University of British Columbia and Emily Carr Institute of Art and Design respectively.

Patrik Andersson (Vancouver)

Patrik Andersson received his Ph.D. from the University of British Columbia with a dissertation on Marcel Duchamp entitled *Euro-Pop: The Mechanical Bride Stripped Bare in Stockholm, Even*. He teaches critical studies at Emily Carr Institute of Art and Design and has published numerous texts and curated exhibitions on contemporary and historical art. He is also the director and curator of Trapp Gallery in Vancouver, Canada. In 2000 he co-curated (with Derek Root & Judith Steedman) the exhibition *Supersonic Transport: A Survey of Independent Pop Culture Magazines*.

Beyond Magazines

Patrik Andersson

Objects are to me only material that I use up. Wherever I put my hand I grasp a truth, which I trim for myself. The truth is certain to me, and I do not need to long after it. To do the truth a service is in no case my intent; it is to me only a nourishment for my thinking head, as potatoes are for my digesting stomach, or as a friend is for my social heart. As long as I have the humor and force for thinking, every truth serves me only for me to work it up according to my powers.

Max Stirner, 1845[1]

Before trying to distinguish the epic side of modern life, and before bringing examples to prove that our age is no less fertile in sublime themes than the past ages, we may assert that since all centuries and all peoples have had their own form of beauty, so inevitably we have ours. The pageant of fashionable life and the thousands of floating existences—criminals and kept women—which drift about in the underworld of a great city; the *Gazette des Tribunaux* and the *Moniteur* all prove to us that we have only to open our eyes to recognize our heroism.

Charles Baudelaire, 1846[2]

Unlike most of the young Hegelians he was hanging out with in the Berlin beerhalls of the 1840s, Saint Max, as Marx and Engels called Stirner, only managed to publish one book of his own, but it ended up saying what few other philosophers, politicians or teachers of his day dared to say. It suggested that the world as we know it is made up. "Truth" is really nothing but an elaborate hoax—a myth. What's more, Stirner suggested that if the world is in fact constructed, it can also be deconstructed and rebuilt into an image of your own.

Just a year after Stirner's book hit the shelves of some obscure bookstores in Berlin, on what must have have been a particularly sunny and optimistic afternoon in Paris, Charles Baudelaire, in a review of that city's annual salon, proposed a similar idea to his readers. Baudelaire argued that contemporary experiences of everyday life were just as significant to represent in text and images as the official demand the Academy had for classical representations of war, biblical passages or ridiculously mythologized portraits. He proposed that if you wanted to be a truly *modern* artist, not only would your subjects be well dressed (i.e., not wear togas and past military regalia) but they would also be well represented *in their times*. Rather than hide your subjects in the past, the artist should think seriously enough about his or her world to realize that a new form of beauty and heroism existed that was rooted in fleeting moments whose impressions could be captured and transformed into your own history. Baudelaire, in other words, decided to represent *his own* world. Significantly, in this new, at first imagined, social order, public participation would shift from a dependence on good breeding to a knowledge and display of good behaviour. In this new and distinctly bourgeois world, social interaction, rather than family lineage, was starting to forge a new type of public urban space. It was time to dress up.

Berlin and Paris were of course not the first nor the last places to witness this kind of social transformation. By the mid-18th century, domestic patterns of consumption in London had shifted so much as to allow the lower classes to start buying goods previously considered luxuries. The anxiety created by this gradual class-leveling in England was described by some as "genteel mania."[3] In these and other cities, commerce was creating a more privatized society, to the point that traditional civic virtues were rapidly becoming outmoded and challenged. More and more, people were gaining access to power. As Baudelaire, Stirner and others were beginning to realize, a structural transformation of the public sphere could take place only if, alongside economic and military control, representation was harnessed. Even if it wasn't necessarily sunny in Paris the day Baudelaire wrote his review arguing for a modern representation, it is empowering to think that his optimism could see through the clouds of his day to provide his readers with a potential clearing where they could write their own history.

As Uscha Pohl describes in her contribution to this book, "it is Marcel Duchamp in 1945 who earns himself the medal of being the first sole artist to create and design his magazine, *VIEW*, entirely autonomously, ringing in a new era, a new point of view." Considering the fact that Duchamp claims Stirner is the only philosopher to have directly influenced his work, *VIEW* can perhaps be seen as a 100th anniversary celebration of *The Ego and His Own*. For Duchamp and other artists after him, the *idea* of a magazine would function as a means to challenge and play with a perceived gap between popular culture and high art.

With the advent of home computers and programs like the ones Judith and I have used to make this book, more and more people are discovering ways and reasons to produce their own magazine. In fact, at a moment when some had predicted that print culture would be replaced by a digital landscape of information highways, there are more magazines (and books) being produced than ever before.

But is this plethora of pulp necessarily good? In an editorial statement accompanying the Dutch publication *OHNO Another Magazine*, graphic designer Armand Mevis poignantly sums up the way many of us feel about the magazine industry at this stage in history:

> As a reader, I am not really interested in magazines. Week after week, month after month, the popular magazine publishers try to seduce us into buying their wares. The content of what you buy doesn't matter because you buy it to confirm, over and again, what you already know. The same subjects crop up repeatedly in the same magazines. They follow the trivia of the glamorous and famous and keep us informed about what they are up to, where and with whom. A newly published magazine does its best to stand out as unique, but after a few issues, it invariably becomes obvious that the advertisers, not the editors, pull the strings.[4]

Yet, despite this deterministic view, Mevis and other individuals around the globe insist on producing new forms of publications, which strive toward independent editorial control. This book has been produced to acknowledge this sign of life and suggest that a publishing genre located in-between the world of underground zines and more mainstream magazines had manifested itself as a prominent trend by the turn of the century. Designers, artists and writers continue to make visible their interest in this genre, which remains undefined but is recognizable by its hybrid character and limited circulation.

Rarely are these "hyzines" produced with the intention of generating more money than it costs for them to exist. More attention is given to specific editorial details (subject and design) and a commitment to a dedicated audience. Probing the content of publications such as *Re-* (Netherlands), *Ref.* (Japan), *Purple* (France) and *VERY* (United States), our aim has been to make visible both connections and differences within design and editorial strategies. One of the strongest links between all these publications is the continued interest in making an "other" magazine. Within today's globalized economy of signs, the ability to make unique design and editorial decisions is increasingly circumscribed. As Mevis points out, there is the pressure exercised by advertising to not stray too far outside a mainstream consumer culture. Attempts to establish and maintain an "independent" position that stands out in this visual and conceptual field usually succeed in doing so for only a brief moment in time as their dialects become absorbed and homogenized into mass culture.

The precarious space individual editors operate in often mirrors the artistic activities of a modernist and avant-garde endgame. Rather than trying to be modernist or postmodern, the publications included in this book respond to a sense of "post-ideology" in which repeating the experiences of modern life becomes the only means to claim an active and conscious position.[5] Produced *now* and *here*, these nomadic cultural expressions locate an "in-between" space and recognize their peripheral positions as *nowhere*.

But nowhere is where it's at! After all, it is on this periphery that the strategies of avant-garde art continue to meet the latest developments in popular culture. If artists have consistently returned to this edge to get a new perspective on urban modernity, pop cultural "losers" like Beck have equally appropriated the language of the everyday. In either case, new representational strategies have been employed to make public local and global lifestyles. As the material in this book suggests, the individuals in this constantly made public sphere often share a pictorial vocabulary that is neither unique nor naïve.

It should not come as a surprise that the majority of the photographs and illustrations in these publications have the "look" of contemporary art. As Jeff Rian has suggested, "nowadays everyone is a 'kind of' artist, too, and privy to insider knowledge; styles of representation have entered the mazy world of subtexts and metamessages ("meta" meaning beyond)." In magazines ranging in scope from *Sec.* to *Visionaire*, metamessages find their most common ground in the medium of photography, which by the '90s had also established itself as a dominant artistic medium in the art world. This rise to aesthetic, intellectual and economic importance resulted from a variety of modernist approaches to the medium. Whether "snapshot" or "straight," the documentary nature of photography was employed to various degrees by artists as diverse as Nan Goldin, Thomas Ruff, Jack Pierson, Nobuyoshi Araki and Reneke Dijkstra, who found diverse ways to approach quotidian life in a self-reflexive manner. It is this interest in the everyday that establishes an important intersection between these independent publications and the world of art, design, music and fashion.

Jeff Wall has suggested that there is a "liquid intelligence" behind the photographic print that allows it to be used in an historical and self-conscious manner.[6] Wall calls up the relationship between the mechanically "dry" institution of the medium and this "liquid" process that has as much to do with the medium as it does with the individual maker. Photography is thus "archaic" insofar as it "embodies a memory-trace" of the creative act. For Wall, the hubris of new technologies increasingly presents a threat to creative self-reflection as it expands the dry part of the medium in ways that displace the liquid process. In many ways this parallels the precarious position of these publications, which are attempting to hold on to the experience of making "slicks" for a limited audience in a publishing industry mass-marketing "glossies" for a general audience. While the latter follow axiomatic flows, the former set out to negotiate and define individual movement within mainstream culture by responding to regional pop cultural desires. The repetitious nature of this process is simultaneously new and archaic but always striving to be creative.

The process just described is not limited to photography alone. All these publications rely on illustrations and graphic design that try to be creative without claiming originality. Just as there is a predominant theme of in-between spaces, the periphery and awkward teenagers in the photographs, the balance of puerile, naïve and earnestly drawn illustrations calls up a similar state of transition. Dialoguing with Karen Kilimnik's diaristic teenage obsessions and Elizabeth Peyton's documentary self-portraits as her music idols, the illustrations often shuttle between subjects of adolescence, adulthood, obscurity and limelight. Equally mimetic, the graphic design is often located somewhere between the gridded rationalism of Swiss design and the naïve awkwardness of first-time desktop publishing. In all instances, the selection of paper and printing method is carefully thought out to give the reader/viewer the right "feel."

Although this genre of magazines exemplifies cutting-edge publishing trends in the last decade, there are many predecessors, a few of which are discussed in this book's other essays. Often spawned from within the art scene, the very early issues of Warhol's *Interview* magazine and General Idea's *FILE* are good examples from the '60s and '70s of publications produced to siphon mainstream culture through avant-garde strategies of mimetics, irony and humor. These and a few other magazines such as *After Dark, i-D, The Face* and *Hype* were all attempts to to visualize and make public (in the limited sense of that word) desires emerging from difference and collaboration rather than sameness and collectivity. Cultural theorist Dick Hebdige has noted that in the '80s *The Face* provided a:

> set of physical cultural resources that young people [could] use in order to make some sense and get some pleasure out of growing up in an increasingly daunting and complex environment. It has been instrumental in shaping an emergent structure of feeling, a 1980s sensibility as distinctive in its own right as that of the late 1960s.[8]

For the producers of the magazine, importance was placed on editorial control of design, which resulted from a great deal of personal funding. Nick Logan, publisher of *The Face*, noted in 1985 (at the height of the Thatcher era) that his magazine was "quite self indulgent. I wanted it to be monthly so that you were out of that weekly rut; on glossy paper so that it would look good; and with very few ads— at *NME* the awful shapes of ads often meant that you couldn't do what you wanted with the design."[8]

While *The Face* and publications such as *Interview* have predictably since their inception been put on autopilot and turned into more corporate mainstream investments, there continue to emerge magazines that re-enact the allegorical conflict between individual and mass cultural desires. The aim of this book has been to shed light on a selection of magazines from around the world that continue to play this game of representation.

Note: A slightly different version of this text appeared in a catalogue accompanying the exhibition *Supersonic Transport: A Survey of Independent Pop Culture Magazines*, organized by the Charles H. Scott Gallery for Emily Carr Institute of Art and Design, Vancouver, the Netherlands Design Institute, Amsterdam, and the Dunlop Art Gallery, Regina.

1   Max Stirner, *The Ego and His Own* (London: Modern Library, no date [originally published in 1845 in Munich]).

2   Charles Baudelaire, "The Salon of 1846: On the Heroism of Modern Life," reprinted in *Modern Art and Modernism: A Critical Anthology*, edited by Francis Frascina and Charles Harrison (New York: Harper & Row Publishers), 1983, pp. 17-18.

3   David Solkin, *Painting for Money: The Visual Arts and the Public Sphere in Eighteenth Century England* (New Haven: Yale University Press, 1992).

4   Armand Mevis, "Editorial: On Magazines," *OHNO Another Magazine* (Maastricht: Jan van Eyck Akademie, 1999), p. 1.

5   With post-ideology I am not suggesting that ideology has disappeared but rather that its politics have shifted into a more ambiguous territory of experience. This was recently the subject of a large art exhibition held at Moderna Museet in Stockholm, curated by Pier Luigi Tazzi and David Elliott. See David Elliott's "No Pain, No Gain" in *Wounds: Between Democracy and Redemption in Contemporary Art* (Stockholm: Moderna Museet, 1998).

6   Jeff Wall, "Liquid History of Photography," reprinted in *Jeff Wall* (London: Phaidon, 1998).

7   Dick Hebdige, "The Bottom Line on Planet One: Squaring Up to the Face," in *Hiding in the Lights: On Images and Things* (London: Routledge, 1988), p. 155.

8   *Ibid.*

A Select
Survey of
Independent
Pop Culture
Magazines

Adbusters

Animal Stories

Asianpunkboy

Bibel

Butt

Catalogue

Ghost Stories

Hot Rod

Index

Kit & Caboodle

Lab

List

Mall Punk

McSweeney's

Merge

Permanent Food

Petit Glam

Purple

Re-

Ref.

Sec.

VERY

Visionaire

all images and text pages 22-117
courtesy individual magazines

Adbusters

Based: Vancouver, Canada
Editor: Kalle Lasn
www.adbusters.org

Adbusters *magazine, launched in 1989 by editor Kalle Lasn, was the first to challenge popular culture on its own turf—using the techniques and machinery of advertising and the mass media to sell ideas rather than products, to subvert rather than promote, to create cognitive dissonance rather than brand loyalty. It was among the first to identify the glut of commercial messages as an "environmental" problem. To a consumer culture choked by the commodification and corporatization of absolutely everything, it proposes big, structural changes: from the way TV stations are run to the way the human body is "sold" to the way economists measure progress.*

Adbusters *is a locus for the actions, ideas and aspirations of a global network of artists, writers, activists, pranksters, philosophers, musicians poets and punks. To these self-declared culture jammers, the most potent revolutionary tool is the meme—the image, buzzword, tactic or idea that can spread throughout a culture and shape the way we see our world.*

ADBUSTERS

No.37

SPECIAL DOUBLE ISSUE.

DESIGN ANARCHY

US/CAN $7.95 UK £4.50 ¥1500

05

7 78624 79265 5

vol. 9 no. 5
sept/oct 2001

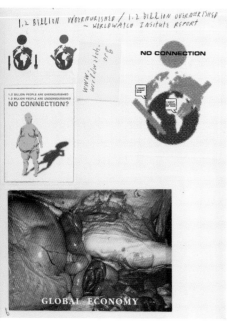

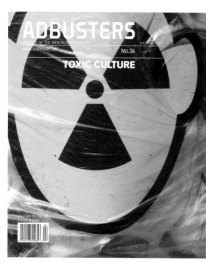

The only predictable thing in the Situationist City would be its unpredictability, its random intensity, its unity of ambience.

— Guy Debord

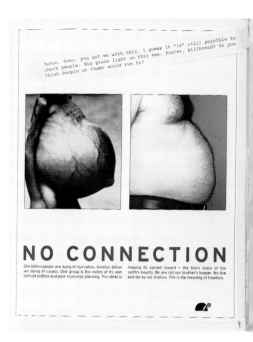

Jesus, Kono, you got me with this. I guess it *is* still possible to shock people. Big green light on this one. Poster, billboard? Do you think People or Cosmo would run it?

NO CONNECTION

One billion people are dying of starvation. Another billion are dying of excess. One group is the victim of its own corrupt politics and poor economic planning. The other is reaping its earned reward — the lion's share of the earth's bounty. We are not our brother's keeper. We live and die by our choices. This is the meaning of freedom.

ADBUSTERS

JOURNAL OF THE MENTAL ENVIRONMENT >> MAR/APR 2001 >> NO. 34

US/CAN $5.95
UK £3.50 ¥1200

love

>> return home?
>> y/n

Animal Stories

Based: Los Angeles
Editor: Casey McKinney
Design: Matthew Greene and Casey McKinney
www.animalstories.net

When I first came up with the idea to make Animal Stories, I had no idea of what I was get-
ting into. I printed business cards, made a crappy web site and went to everyone I could think
of, from friends and relatives to galleries in Atlanta and Europe, and asked them if they
would contribute to this hypothetical thing. I became sort of gibberishly obsessed with the idea,
grandiosely formulating in my head a business plan and manifesto to rival the late JFK Jr.'s,
while relishing a kind of perverse pleasure whenever people I solicited laughed at the thought
of writing an animal story. How boring and cute it all seemed. But the final product I believe
was quite different. Not boring, I would like to think, and certainly not cute. With the help
of the faithful, those who contributed and those who aided in design and distribution, a real
magazine emerged. A full-color, completely non-commercial, almost fiscally viable magazine.
A rarity, it now seems.

Animal Stories Magazine

Issue 1 Spring 2000 $6 US

Clairvoyant

Dallas Hudgens

Once, on the night after Christmas, my mother asked me to ride around town with her to take one last look at the lights on the houses.

"Come on," she said, "be my handsome date."

I was fourteen at the time. I didn't want to go with her. But it was late, and she had been drinking grocery-store Eggnog and Jack Daniel's. I thought she might need me to grab the wheel at some point in the drive. It had happened before.

She picked out a subdivision and started to barrel her way through it. She was working on a Pall Mall and driving so fast you would have thought she was trying to blow out the Christmas lights instead of admire them. She never looked right to me with a cigarette in her mouth. She always looked nervous, like a girl who was worried about being caught.

"What a letdown," she said between drags. "Don't you think this is the worst day of the year? All that buildup, and then one tremendous letdown."

I told her I guessed she was right, but I didn't really mean it. I already knew that you had to eye every day of the year with a good bit of wariness.

"I'm thinking of calling Louis when we get back to the apartment," she said. "What do you say we drive down to Pensacola for a few days and see old Louie, Louie?"

"I thought Louie stole your car and wrecked it the last time you saw him."

"That car was a piece of shit, anyway," she said. "Besides, it's the season of forgiveness. It's in the air. Unto this world, a child is born in Bethlehem, in a manger far away to give forgiveness to all, even to a sack of shit like Louie."

The car needed some sanity from the outside world. I leaned over and fiddled with the radio tuner, but nothing would come in. Not even static. The only sound in the car was the heater fan. It clattered away like it always did, blowing warm air that smelled of fast food burgers.

"All right," my mother said. "He's an asshole. I'll grant you that. But don't you just want to get out of here for a while, take in a change of scenery? I mean it's Pensacola, for Christ sake. It's the beach. Everybody likes going to the beach. At least we'll have a free place to stay."

I didn't want to sleep on Louie's air mattress or smell his cat's litter box or go to a bar to hear his band play their twenty-minute version of "Low Rider." That wasn't my idea of an escape. I had four days until school started back, and I wanted to spend a good portion of that time at my girlfriend's house, sliding my hand up under her sweater while she pretended to watch *All My Children.*

"What about work?" I asked my mother.

"I'll tell them I had a family emergency," she said. "Screw 'em. They can fire me if they want, but I'm not spending all week writing up exchange receipts. I've done that song and dance, helping out all the ungrateful people in the world, returning every gift they get and wanting to know if they can exchange it for cash."

She had worked at the mall for as long as I could remember, selling clothes to women who had new houses and car radios that never went on the blink. She was always quitting or getting fired from one store or another, but her regular customers were always willing to follow her to the next stop. Maybe they thought she could make them look as good as she looked in those clothes. She was thirty-four years old then. But when she put on a baby blue sweater set and a grey flannel skirt, she could pass for a girl right out of college. Blonde hair. Blue eyes. Little dimples in her cheeks. And a smile that could sell.

But she wasn't selling me on the trip to Pensacola.

18

"I'm not going," I said.

"What do you mean, you're not going?"

"I'm just not," I said. "Why don't you plan something ahead of time, for a change. Maybe you wouldn't have to call assholes like Louie for a place to stay."

She slowed down and turned and looked at me with her mouth open. In the green light from the dash she looked older. I could even see wrinkles, carved from all those years of narrowing her eyes around cigarette smoke and disappointment. The sight of her face made me feel older myself, or at least what I thought that being older might feel like. I wanted to run away, maybe with my girlfriend. But not to Pensacola.

I waited for my mother to say something. I think I wanted her to say that I was right, that what she'd been talking about was foolishness. I wanted her to say that she was going to plan a real trip, and we'd drive up to the mountains to ski some weekend. She'd say that she was going to keep her job this time and try to get a management position so we could rent a house somewhere and not have to worry about peeping toms or the fellow who stalked the woman in the apartment above ours. She'd say she was going to take that stack of Home and Garden magazines beside her bed and put them to good use. I knew that she liked ferns and dahlias and those big stone bird baths. She'd also told me once about how she and her grandfather had painted his house together one summer. It was the summer before he died. She said she'd always wanted to do that again.

But before she could say anything, a dog scampered out in front of the car. It was a little beagle with a silver collar, and it came out of nowhere. It just stood there with its red eyes locked onto the high beams.

"Whoa!" I said. "Look out!"

I reached over and grabbed the wheel, but my mother was already thinking along the same lines. We both jerked the car over the center line. When we did it, the dog moved with us. We sawed the wheel back to the right, and again the dog followed us. It was like the headlights had cast some sort of spell on the dog.

We were about to clip a brick mailbox, so we whipped the car back off the shoulder. This time we ran right over the dog. We caught it with the right front tire.

"Oh, God," my mother said. "I think I hit him."

She stopped the car and let it idle in the middle of the road. I checked the side mirror and saw the beagle lying on its side. One of its hind legs was twitching in the air.

"Did I kill it?" my mother said. "Did I kill it? Please don't tell me I killed it."

She had her forehead resting on the steering wheel and her hands still planted at three and nine.

"He's moving," I said. "I can see him moving his leg. Maybe we just stunned him a little."

But I knew we hadn't stunned the dog. I knew it was much worse than that. I knew that little beagle had pranced across its last green lawn.

Animal Stories Magazine 19

The Bear Trap

by E. Andrew Bennett

I was walking one night in the arctic across the hard crust of glazed snow. My boots left no track behind me and the flat mantle swept out in all directions so to give the impression of a hugely wide and smooth floor of marble. My footsteps kept rigid cadence with my breath and nothing else moved or made a sound in the vastly horizontal space. The camp was still about 15 miles distant, but I was not concerned as the weather was clear and mild and if it hadn't been nighttime, I could probably have seen it from where I was, so desolate was the landscape. Keeping a brisk pace, I was comfortable, if not warm, and loosened my hood and coat, removing my facemask and goggles without the adversity to which I'd become accustomed. Indeed, that strange night, many of the cautions one retains in such hard climates seemed no longer necessary. The moon was bright enough that I could read my compass by it, and I estimated that by the time the sun rose, I would easily be within a mile of my destination. Its blackness, standing out in such great contrast with the rest of the world, was impossible to miss. The serenity of that rare arctic night made the walk even relaxing and I felt it would be almost a religious adventure of the kind I had been wanting for some time. It was an opportunity to reflect on my life and the human state such that I was actually glad my jeep and radio had failed me.

I had not been but a few miles along on my journey when I noticed a tiny movement in the distance. Continuing on my way, while casually occupying myself by squinting in its direction, my footsteps came to an abrupt halt and a chill of recognition gripped my chest so that my breath stopped and I confronted a fear. I could clearly see across the frost some 500 yards to my left the horrific loping form of Thalarctos maritimus, the bear in its arctic presentation. A bear is a creature of some danger wherever found, but especially dangerous is this larger and less trustworthy variety, as it is not accustomed to predation in its own hostile environment. My first instinct was to remain perfectly motionless and to allow it to simply slip by on its nightly forage unaware of my presence. But no sooner had I stopped than it stopped and I knew that all this time while I was lost in the arctic's lonely majesty I was not alone but being followed. I stepped forward, marking its movements with my eye as we walked again together at my strictly kept pace. At five minutes I estimated we had covered one third of a mile, or roughly 587 yards. During which time it seemed to my discomfort to have come about a tenth the distance nearer, or about 58 yards. It was traveling a path almost parallel to mine, but one that slowly closed the distance so that we might intersect at a point some three miles on or so. This made my hope of reaching camp without a conflict futile. It was at this point I remembered abandoning my rifle, wanting to be as unencumbered as possible, in the jeep about three and a third miles behind me. At our current trajectories, allowing for conservative error, I could forseeably make the jeep, at 1760 times three point three...5808 yards behind me losing 58 times 3, or 174 yards between us for every mile meaning we would connect at maybe 450 divided by 174, about 2.6 miles? Looking the situation over as quickly as possible, realizing the more time spent calculating the closer we came to each other and the further I went from the jeep, I reevaluated the bear's distance from me at maybe 550 yards, bringing the point of our meeting at 3.16, or just past the third mile. With maybe a little sprint at the end of our hike I could do it.

This was of course, assuming that the act of suddenly stopping and reversing direction did nothing to interfere with the bear's pattern, and also that the bear's pattern itself was constant and immutable. A bear's behavior cannot be predicted, true, not every encounter ends in a fatality. It may just be playing a game. Maybe issuing me an exam of some sort to test my strength or cunning. Or it could be lonely in this bleak and icy world, in which case I should just pass along my way. But I couldn't work with the bear being variable so I had to make it constant.

Better yet, I could set out toward the jeep at an angle some degrees to the right of it. And clipping the angle by arcing slightly, I could drift to the left some 50 yards to the mile, undetectable to the bear but giving me almost an extra 50 times three, 150 as compared to 174, one mile to work with. But then the extra distance that must be crossed by arcing may eat up all my advantage. I looked to my compass. How many degrees right of my target would be 150 yards at three miles? I could not perform the calculation in my head so I made an abrupt turn and set out walking some 30 degrees to the right of where my jeep was left, in the direction of the bear. Planning to shift my path one degree to the left every tenth of a mile, or about every minute and a half. I watched the bear's reaction carefully. It sat still for a moment watching me walk away and then, after perhaps two minutes, or approximately 235 yards, abruptly reared up and bounded to the area I had just left, crossing it and settling at an almost equal distance as before on the opposite side. Again it began keeping my pace, still to my left but this time, however, between me and the jeep. Any arcing done now would be toward the beast, bringing the point of our meeting almost a mile nearer. The only way out, I reasoned, was to arc hard in the opposite direction, making an eventual circle ending in the vicinity of the abandoned vehicle. Again, my abilities could not perform the equation I formed so clearly in my head. The need for a new focus brought such ambiguity into things that a guess seemed almost as accurate. So I set off in a slight curve I reasoned would circle my pursuer and bring me to my weapon while there was still space between us.

It was only a matter of minutes before I was completely disoriented. I did not fail, though, to continue generally placing myself on the mental map I'd made of the area by watching the stars and my watch, and I kept a steady pace. We walked in this manner for 42 minutes, 2.8 miles. As predicted the bear now was unnervingly close, about 200 yards to my left. My path should form a spiral with a length of about a third the circumference of a circle with a radius of 5808 yards, or 3.14 times 5808 squared. There's no way that could possibly be right. Damn my head. I was getting irritated, the bear closing steadily as I continually altered my path, when a sudden wind came over us bringing an intense cloud of flurries, so dense that all visual cues and even the bear itself were obscured. With increasing uneasiness I replaced my facemask and goggles and continued blindly. In the flying snow and darkness I could make out neither my watch nor compass. So disconnected with every object of my advantage, surely I would be doomed I thought in such wretched conditions as no natural thing could possibly conceal me. The more I considered my situation, the more I began to despair.

Hopelessly, weary and fearful, I walked on for what could have been hours or minutes, blindly putting one foot before the other when at last I was compelled by the impossibility of my task and the new found hope that maybe my pursuer, too, was likewise beguiled by the flying snow and wind and was now miles away that I stopped to rest, dropping to my knees in the snow. Pleasingly, the flurries soon abated and the last of the wind and stinging particles of ice siphoned away leaving the air still again but colder than indeed still air had ever felt before. I wiped my goggles and looked around in amazement at where I found myself. Towering on all sides around me, gigantic against the landscape, stood a circle of huge upright stones, about 25 feet high, and while not cut so cleanly, smoothed and pitted enough by the active weather as to appear unscalable. There were nine in all, each about eight feet wide with an equal space between them. My mind raced at the methods and meanings of their construction. So many questions arose. What was it? What ancient peoples were responsible? How had they come here and how had this strange and obvious place, apparently so near the camp, remained unfound?

All questions were forgot with the next sight to come. From around one of the monoliths, standing erect and silhouetted blue by the moon and reaching a height over 12 feet tall, stepped the polar bear. It stood wavering in the clean icy air and fell to its haunches before me, crushing the ground where it fell, extending its long and wide head, fangs bared and growling. I jumped to my feet as it lunged forward. Everything about it was power and I was motion. I ducked quickly behind the nearest stone as it tumbled past. Rushing behind another stone while it prepared its second charge, I easily moved aside and hid myself. Again it dove by. The third time it approached slowly and I waited. As it came nearer I turned the corner and ran around the stone's base so that I was at the bear's rear before it had cleared the first corner. It turned toward me and I reversed the move, standing again behind it. This time, more irritated, it lunged, clumsily throwing its mass clear out of the circle. Taking advantage of the bought time I attempted to scramble up the stones, but it was impossible. They were too sheer and glossed with ice and my clothes were too bulky. I dashed instead to clear the diameter with the bear right behind me, stepping behind a stone on the other side in time to see the beast careen past and slowly turn to gallop back, wagging its broad head mightily. I laughed out loud. Out on the open expanse of snow there was certainly no escape, but around this old and weathered structure there were unlimited ways to avoid being eaten, if also no escape. And there was no need for calculations. The mathematics was so simple. It was automatic. And I am alive to this day through this simple contraption. Though to this day I am still out on that arctic plain, avoiding being eaten. Unable to escape.

64

Animal Stories Magazine 65

Fábula filosófica de los pequeños animales

Benito del Pliego
(illustrations by Osvaldo Razo)

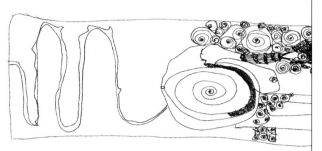

Habla la mosca:

— «La insistencia es virtud y condena. Reincidir en lo que se ama puede con razón parecer un desvarío. Solo quien insiste hace de su ruina salvación. El hambre es una fuerza pequeña en opinión del obseso. El frío se acepta; pero la insatisfacción es un cuchillo que se clava uno mismo. El mundo es pequeño y miserable pero el deseo lo transforma en un panal y él nos sacia y nos hace gozar, y nos atrapa y nos entierra»

Habla la ardilla:

— «Que la vida debe ser tomada en serio es verdad que está por aceptarse. Unos miran el árbol y ven en él una columna formidable que une el cielo y la tierra. Yo solo sé que un árbol está lleno de avellanas. Reírse a tiempo y a la cara no solo fortalece sino que a otros da motivos para el odio, afecto más ameno que la contemplación y el sueño. Desenterrar lo que plantaste en los jardines y exponer los cables a la lluvia son anticipo de un broma mayor y que a todos nos incluye»

Habla la rana:

— «Quien vive a la orilla del agua repite siempre el mismo canto. Un solo sonido es suficiente. La salmodia de una gota abriéndose constante entre los círculos es eco capaz de hacer a cada uno oírse. No vale tampoco la pena dejarse llevar por el ansia de cruzar el mundo. Para viajar ya basta con traspasar una línea. Tierra y agua se solapan y sin embargo encierran dos mundos separados, así como lo son madurez e infancia»

Habla la hormiga:

— «Todo lo grande lo forman las cosas pequeñas, que encierran a su vez inmensas dimensiones. No hay nada en la tierra que no sea hormiga, si bien yo sé mejor que nadie que cada cosa es ella y solo ella misma. Mis patas son yo y la hilera que bulle en el tronco del árbol también lo es, y las galerías subterráneas en que el pulgón amamanta a mis crías (que son yo misma), y el grano de trigo que almaceno en su interior y he comido mil veces, y la arena que aparto y donde muero y la hoja de rosal que recorta mi compañera. Ya sé que no es sencillo, algunos tenemos perfiles complejos que el ojo no puede ver ni la cabeza comprende. Pero qué importa, ceguera e ignorancia son otras formas de mi ser»

The fly speaks:

— Persistence is a virtue and a sentence. To relapse into that which one loves can, it is true, seem an absurdity. Only he who persists turns his ruin into his salvation. Hunger means little to the obsessed. Cold can be accepted too, but dissatisfaction is a knife that one uses to stab oneself. The world is small and miserable but desire transforms it into a beehive, and it satiates us, and gives pleasure, and traps us, and buries us.

The squirrel speaks:

— That life should be taken seriously is a debatable truth. Some look at the tree and see a formidable column that brings together heaven and earth. I just know that a tree is full of acorns. To laugh at time and at someone's face not only makes you stronger but also gives others reasons to hate, a more pleasant feeling than contemplation and dream. To unearth what you planted in the gardens and to expose the wires to the rain is only an anticipation of a bigger joke that includes us all.

The frog speaks:

— He who lives at the water's edge always repeats the same song. One single sound is enough. The monotonous sound of a drop constantly opening itself among the circles is an echo capable of making each one hear itself. It is not worth letting the anxiety of crossing the world take over. To travel, it is enough to go through a line. Earth and water overlap each other and yet enclose two separate worlds, like maturity and infancy.

The ant speaks:

— Every big thing is formed by littler ones that enclose immense dimensions. There is nothing on earth that is not an ant, even I know better than anyone that every single thing is itself and nothing but itself. My legs are me, and the row that moves across the trunk of the tree is also me, and the subterranean tunnels where the plant louse suckles my young (who are also myself), and the wheat that I store inside and that I have eaten thousands of times, and the sand that I remove and where I die, and the leaf of the rosebush that my companion cuts. I know, it is not easy; some of us have a complicated profile which the eye cannot see nor the head understand. But what does it matter, blindness and ignorance are other forms of my being.

Animal Fashion

31

Asianpunkboy

Based: Vancouver/New York
Art-Direction/Design: Terence Koh
Deputy Art Director: Miguel da Conceicao
www.asianpunkboy.com

ASIANPUNKBOY *Magazine chronicles the real experience of a real asian punk boy cyber-hustler. A printed journal filled with an infusion of gentle surfaces, dissidents, haikus, and mapped pictures...*

For the first issue of ASIANPUNKBOY 01: *The Empty City, 35 artists have contributed work including Richard Prince, Ryan McGinley, Stephen Sprouse and fashion designers ORFI, United Bamboo, Bruce La Bruce and Benjamin Cho.*

ASIANPUNKBOY *in a limited edition of only 200, comes in three books; Landscapes, Conversations and Journeys.*

The books are united by 200 different fabric covers, guest-designed by various artists.

Right: Cover by ASIANPUNKBOY *and Dimitri Joseph*

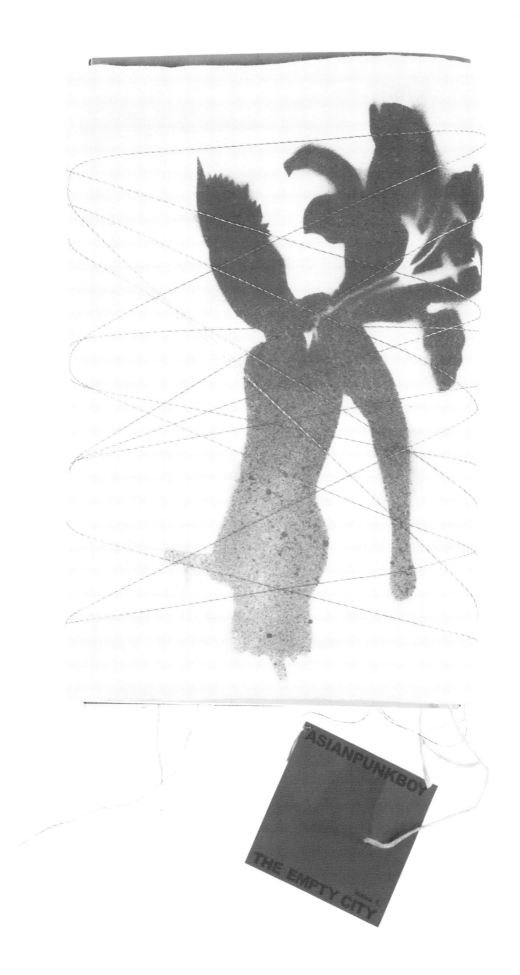

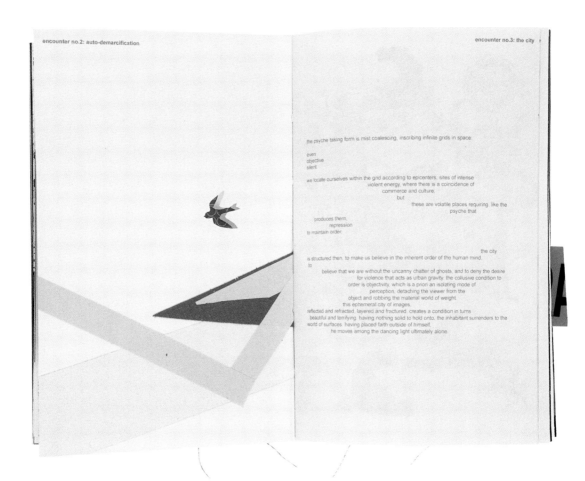

the psyche taking form is mist coalescing, inscribing infinite grids in space.

even
objective
silent

we locate ourselves within the grid according to epicenters, sites of intense
violent energy, where there is a coincidence of
commerce and culture;
but
these are volatile places requiring, like the
psyche that
produces them,
repression
to maintain order.

the city
is structured then, to make us believe in the inherent order of the human mind,
to
believe that we are without the uncanny chatter of ghosts, and to deny the desire
for violence that acts as urban gravity. the collusive condition to
order is objectivity, which is a priori an isolating mode of
perception, detaching the viewer from the
object and robbing the material world of weight.
this ephemeral city of images,
reflected and refracted, layered and fractured, creates a condition in turns
beautiful and terrifying; having nothing solid to hold onto, the inhabitant surrenders to the
world of surfaces. having placed faith outside of himself,
he moves among the dancing light ultimately alone.

Bibel

Based: Stockholm
Creative Director/Art Director: Stefania Malmsten
Fashion Editor: Maria Ben Saad
Editors: Martin Gelin, Anna Hellsten, Martin Jönsson,
Andres Lokko, Annina Rabe, Fredrik Strage
Photographers: Terese Andrén, Ola Bergengren, Anders Edström, J.H. Engström,
Irmelie Krekin, Andreas Larsson, Ola Rindal, Camilla Åkrans
Stylists: Ann-Sofie Back, Mattias Karlsson, Robert Rydberg,
Yoshiko Shiojiri, Sally O'Sullivan
Illustrators: Lovisa Burfitt, Paul Davis, Patrick Long, Stina Johnson,
Kristian Russell, Liselotte Watkins, Vår

Bibel was launched in March 1998 and came out with 15 issues until April 2000. During its short existence, Bibel changed the way people in Sweden look at fashion and also managed to connect with an international audience. Within a pop cultural context Bibel mixed fashion with music, literature and film, exploring the boundaries between different media and cultural categories. Bibel introduced new, young and independent-minded designers, stylists and photographers from Sweden and abroad, and was part of the global generation shift in the fashion world of the late 1990s.

bibel

bättre mode/film/musik/text

Nº 15   april 2000   49 kronor
Norge: 55 nok Finland: 40 fim

Ann-Sofie Back fotograferad av Anders Edström

TIDSAM 0671-15

7 388067 104903

I ♥ **Gutchy**

Looken framför allt.

NIKLAS SAMUELSON/FORTS. snygg klädstil. Inte för att jag skulle klä mig så själv, men han var alltid välklädd och imponerande.

Accessoarer, använder du det?

– Till viss del. Jag gillar pansarlänkar som armband och halsband och nyckelkedja i silver. Scarf brukar jag ha till cowboyskjortor, ja och solglasögon.

Hur ska jeansen vara?

– Jeansen ska vara tillräckligt långa för att man ska kunna vika dem två gånger så att det blir en kant utan avslut. Jag gillar mörk denim, inte jättetight och inte pösigt. Så använder jag byxorna i tre månader tills de är slutkörda.

Hur brett är uppviket på dina jeans?

– 11,5 centimeter.

När du ska vara lite finare, vad har du på fötterna då?

– Då brukar jag ha Saddle Shoes, two-tones, eller några snygga loafers som Hush Puppies eller enfärgade White Bucks eller Black Bucks. Jag ska skaffa ett par riktigt snygga vintagevästernboots också.

Kan du tänka dig att åldras så här?

– Ja, jag vill det, jag hoppas det. Jag trivs så bra i det här. Jag tror att det kommer att dröja länge innan jag byter stil. Sedan vet man inte, man kanske får flint. Då är det bara att lägga ner.

av Maria Lindén

Niklas affär heter East Street Restyling och ligger på Östgötagatan 77, telefon 0709-52 41 00. Lite längre fram i tidningen har han listat årets tatueringar.

Basplagg Nº 7: Tumvanten

Den är inte särskilt praktisk. Du kan inte röka när du har den. Men det är ändå den finaste vanten: tumvanten.

Världens bästa tumvante kommer från... eh, Japan. Det är Final Home, det där konstiga Issey Miyake-sidoprojektet, som ligger bakom den. Det mesta Final Home gör känns lite för mycket Björk-kläder för mig – jag tycker inte att midjeväskor i teflon eller jackor som du kan förvandla till sovsäckar är särskilt kul. Men när de gör något så gammaldags som en tumvante blir det perfekt.

Tumvanten är en gammal plaggform som uppdaterats och det känns som den enda moderna vanten 1999. Den är minimalistisk och funktionell (tumvantar är de varmaste vantarna!). Den ser snäll ut, den ger bra svängrum för fingrarna och den känns tuff.

Martin Gelin

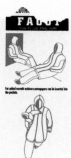

I stället för tumvante från Final Home (design Kosuke Tsumura); en tejpbit med överlevnadskläder.

När Jonas Wiehager var i New York häromsistens fick han lära sig hur man ska snöra sina Nike Dunks: »Det ska se ut som man precis tagit ut dem ur kartongen«, förklarade de som vet. Vi tänkte att ni måste känna till det här om ni planerar att köpa de snygga skorna på bilden härintill.

Album Nº 1: 40° i London

Privatbilder från streetmässan, våren 2000.

Visa röven för Azz, sa Levi's-mannen.

40°-mässan i London var precis som vanligt. Montrarna såg ut som vanligt, och låg till och med på samma ställen. Goldie spelade som vanligt skivor i skateskomontern med sina Metalheadzpolare. Alldeles för stora och tråkiga sko- och klädföretag hade som vanligt alldeles för stora och tråkiga montrar. Och som vanligt sprang alla klädkedjor runt som yra höns och undrade vad som händer nästa säsong. Mode på en mässa som vill vara »on the cutting edge of street fashion« ska inte vara som vanligt. Det ska vara nytt, roligt och spännande. Det här var det enda från mässan som fastnade på min näthinna:

1. Att ett nytt och bra märke som Generic Costume hittade dit.
2. Att svenska Encore, som debuterade på mässan, fick besök av två japaner med tolk som sa hej och köpte in skjortor till 28 butiker i Japan.
3. Att Dope såg bra ut och hade förnyat sig.
4. Paul Franks tjejkollektion.
5. Aem'keis tjejkollektion.
6. Levi's Red-kollektion. Den var riktigt jävla bra, de uppfann jeansen på nytt.
7. En utställning av skatelegenden Mark Gonzales. Det bästa han gjort.

Jonas Wiehager

Färgtant.

Fat white duke. [Jonas själv]

...mässebesökare.

Goldie sportar sitt favoritmärke.

Mark Gonzales-jacka för Levi's Vintage Clothing.

Adidas Kwan.

Tim Burgess, vad har du på dig i dag?

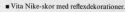

Tim Burgess började sin karriär i neopsykedelia-bandet Electric Crayons, men för tio år sedan slängde han de glittriga skjortorna och blev, som sångare i The Charlatans, Manchester-vågens sötaste pinup-pojke. Nu är han 32 år och bor med sin fru i Los Angeles där han helst shoppar kläder från streetwearmärket J. Crew. Tim tycker att Ol' Dirty Bastard klär sig bättre än någon annan. Och han sjunger lika släpigt och skönt som vanligt på The Charlatans sjätte album »Us and Us Only«.

■ Vita Nike-skor med reflexdekorationer.
– Jag vet inte vad modellen heter, men de är old school. Jag köpte dem i Dallas förra julen. Reflexerna är bra om man är ute och promenerar på natten, men det ser löjligt ut om någon tar en bild av en i mörkret för då lyser skorna som värsta discodojorna.
■ Svarta strumpor.
■ Mörkblå Carhartt-jeans.
– De är sköna, inte speciellt säckiga. Jag köpte ett par Psycho Cowboy-jeans för inte så länge sedan eftersom jag såg ett par i en modetidning. Jag antar att jag är ett modeoffer. Det är fortfarande lika viktigt för mig att hitta häftiga brallor nu som det var för mig att köpa bondage-byxor i tonåren.
■ Tröja från DKNY.
– Jag tror att den är svart. Men det är möjligt att den är blå. Jag blandar ihop de färgerna. Ju äldre jag blir desto mörkare kläder köper jag. För några år sedan försökte jag göra beige coolt igen, men det gick inte.
■ Vita kalsonger med svart kant.
■ Klocka från Kenneth Cole.
■ Halsband med genomskinliga plastkulor från Bloomingdale's i Los Angeles, läderhalsband med stensmycke och ett armband med träkulor.
– Tursmycken som jag fick när jag gifte mig. Jag är rädd för allt ska gå åt helvete om de går sönder.
■ Vigselring i platina med »Forever« ristat på insidan.
– It fuckin' rocks, man.
■ Läppbalsam från Labello.
■ Parfymen Happy från Clinique.
– Jag vet att namnet är lite löjligt men den luktar gott.
■ Vätesuperoxid.
– Jag var trött på mitt gamla hår, så en kväll när jag drack Jack Daniel's och läste en bok om Keith Richards plockade jag fram en flaska blekmedel och gick loss. Jag ville se ut som Keefan gjorde på sjuttiotalet, när han försökte vara lite discoglammig, men det blev bara en löjlig tofs och jag fick blåsor på händerna eftersom jag var asfull och glömde använda handskar.

av Fredrik Strage

Burgess på Hotel Sheraton
ockholm, 12 oktober 1999.

Butt

Based: Amsterdam
Editors: Gert Jonkers and Jop van Bennekom
Email: buttmagazine@xs4all.nl

We started with the word "BUTT" on page one and then we had a long talk with Bas Meerman, whose work makes us smile, and then other people started interviewing other people and Albert made photos of a friend and Peter volunteered to talk with our fave fashion designer Bernhard Willhelm and Wolfgang Tillmans was so kind to shoot him naked and then we wanted to steal back the hot gay iconography that David "bare" Beckham stole from us. And Sico met a colleague artist and there were other guys who we were highly fascinated by like Chris who told us about how he virtually lived on the Internet for quite some months shopping and so on and so on and then SO by Alexander van Slobbe put an ad on page 68 and that's it.

BUTT

Butt Number One
Fag Mag
Spring 2001

PUMA

spijkerbar

**WE WANT IT BECK!
DAVID BECKHAM FOR
ARENA HOMME PLUS
REVISITED**

Fotografie Joy van Hameren
Styling Jos van Hest
Hair & Makeup IR.
Model Lennert

BART JULIUS PETERS FOTOGRAAF DRAAGT VERSACE EN ONTMOET ZONDER BRIL BEROEMDE AMERIKAANSE ACTEUR IN HOMO-SAUNA

door Gert Jonkers
foto Bart Hendriks

Geen opening van een expositie, modeshow of ander art event is compleet zonder Bart Julius Peters, de steevast in pak gestoken, twee meter lange jongeman die dankzij z'n buitensporig model bril en verbaasde blik ook wel 'Bart Bril' of 'Andy Warhol' wordt genoemd. Hij heeft altijd een camera bij zich, maar heeft ooit iemand een foto van zijn hand gezien? Ja. Wie bij Bart Peters op bezoek komt krijgt een grote map vol contactafdrukken op schoot, en daarna een doos vol foto's van chique dames, en een stapel pasfoto's van leuke jongens.

Laten we bij het begin beginnen. Waar je vandaan komt
'Ik ben geboren in Koeweit, mijn vader bouwde er een haven. Daar hebben we tot mijn elfde gewoond, en toen tot mijn twintigste in het Gooi.'

Vandaar die aardappel in je keel?
'Aardappel? Ik vind niet dat ik bekakt praat. Ik praat netjes. Ik kan mijn spraak trouwens prima aan de situatie of 't milieu aanpassen.'

Je bedoelt dat je in bed niet netjes praat?

'In bed praat ik nooit. Of in ieder geval niet veel.'

Heb je kunstacademie gedaan?
'Ja, zeven jaar Rietveld Academie. De eerste drie jaar liep ik daar illegaal rond, want ik werd nooit aangenomen. Een van de docenten zag wel iets in mijn werk dus daarbij mocht ik de lessen volgen zonder dat ik echt op school zat. Daarnaast deed ik de opleiding tekenen en schilderen aan de Lutmastraat. Toen kreeg ik een Braziliaans vriendje en daar ben ik na een half jaar achteraan

Catalogue

Based: Amsterdam
Managing Editor: Winnie Terra
Text Editor: Pauline Terreehorst
Translations: Geoff Salvidant
Graphic Design: goodwill
Email: winnie@cccp.nl
www.ooo.catalogue.nl

As the name suggests, Catalogue is a space dedicated to people who deserve that space, recording the efforts of people who deserve to be recorded. Catalogue has chosen to abuse the current open climate in the arts: each issue has its own guest editor, giving each issue a personal character as he/she may see fit. The open structure of Catalogue only admits that we, the makers, do have an opinion (applied or not) but do not believe our opinion is gospel. We are open to the opinion of all our guests. We hope they can join a discussion based on their and other's opinions in these diffuse times. The broad nature of our guests' ages and backgrounds should bring some varied and inspiring discussions to the surface. Catalogue is not a three-monthly publication. It is an ongoing discussion. Each issue is part of a whole. Catalogue as a series can be bound together to form a catalogue. A unique binder can be ordered from us.

No! I don't know what I'm missing!
(see the back of this card to find out more)

YES! I do/*NO!* I don't* realise that *Catalogue* is a new magazine.
YES! I would/*NO!* I wouldn't* like to know more.
YES! I do/*NO!* I don't* agree that art should lose the capital A.
YES! I do/*NO!* I don't* agree that change brings discussion.
YES! I like/*NO!* I hate* the idea of a guest editor for every issue.
YES! I do/*NO!* I don't* think this could introduce fresh perspectives.
YES! I would/*NO!* I wouldn't* like to be considered as a guest editor.
YES! I do/*NO!* I don't* realise that by doing so I have the freedom to feature one or more artists, whom I feel deserve that much attention for what they have been doing or saying recently.
YES! I do/*NO!* I don't* realise that 'that much attention' is 48 pages.
YES! I do/*NO!* I don't* realise that artist is a vague term.
YES! I do/*NO!* I don't* realise that I must invite others to comment.
YES! I do/*NO!* I don't* realise that all commentary will be published.
YES! I do/*NO!* I don't* have an opinion.
YES! I do/*NO!* I don't* respect everyone else's.

Catalogue

NieuwezijdsVoorburgwal 96
1012 SG Amsterdam
The Netherlands

(*delete do's and don'ts)

(ref: Cat.001. Spring 2001)

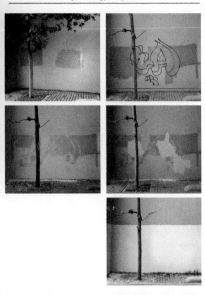

Uw nieuwste vriend, en gastredacteur Gijs Müller:

Ik heb in mijn leven op drie plaatsen gewoond. Mijn jeugd speelde zich af in Lochem, Gelderland. Ik groeide op als in een Zweeds kinderboek: spelen in de bossen, hutten bouwen en slootjespringen, twee broers en twee zussen. Vervolgens ging ik studeren: Enschede, een saaie, middelgrote stad in het Oosten van het land. Ik zat op de kunstacademie, een vrijplaats, een eiland. Ik woonde in een zeepbel. Het contrast tussen de kunstacademie en een dagelijkse ... doen was enorm. Tijdens mijn studie verhuisde ik naar Amsterdam. Het gevoel van vrijheid kreeg hier vleugels. Nu ken ik deze stad en zij kent mij, wij bedienen elkaar. Ik heb geen benul van het gewone wonen. Hoe is dat om op te ...

Catalogue is published quarterly by Stichting Dummy, Amsterdam.

Guest editor for this issue: Gijs Müller
Managing editor: Winnie Terra
Text editor: Pauline Terreehorst
Translations: Geoff Salvidant
Graphic Design: goodwill
Printing: Kwak&VanDaalen&Ronday, Zaandam, NL
Lithography: Edge Pre-media, Weesp, NL

Subscriptions: One year HFL 50,- (Euro 23)
Call: +3120 581 8515 *Mail:* winnie@ccp.nl

Catalogue would not be possible without the kind assistance of all contributors, Tom Meijer, Jaap Ronday, goodwill, Michel de Goede, Geraldo Valken, Rogier vd Ploeg, Rick Smit, Werner Daamen. Without their help and trust, this initiative would not have been possible.

© Stichting Dummy. Images © Photographers
ISSN 1568-4903

Meetpunt, Athens, Maasvlakte

Hoek van Holland

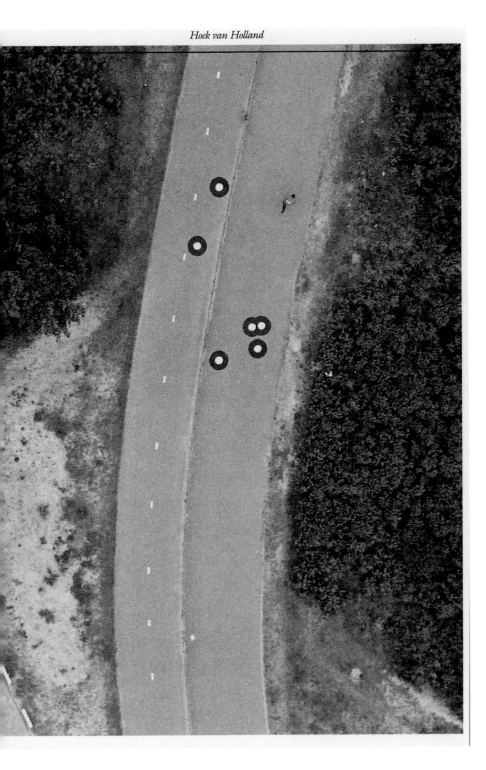

When Paris dissolved into mist it was the blind who showed the aristocracy the way. In the film noir 'Following' by Christopher Nolan (1999) the unemployed writer Bill gets an unexpected guide. Bill follows people as a compensation for the lack of his own life. This tactic backfires on him when he stalks the burglar Cobb. Cobb takes Bill along on a burglary. For Cobb it's not about the act, but about the feeling of snooping around in someone else's house; a fact that certainly touches on the truth. Everyone has heard of the cases in which a thief leaves excrement behind or snacks from the fridge. They have even been known to fry an egg. Cobb goes further. He snuffles around in personal things to get a picture of the occupants of a house, steals one earring so that the owner will learn to value her things again, steals underwear from one house and leaves it behind in another to cause marital problems.

The tour through Rotterdam under the guidance of J. made me think of the film. I - the writer- was towed by the criminal who returned to the scene of the crime. The way in which the burglar in the film "tastefully" steals and influences reality resembles J.'s infiltration in the graffiti and sticker culture. I remained cautious, because things end badly for Bill in the film. Cobb manages, in a very sophisticated way, to trick Bill into the role of accomplice.

suede applications at the shoulder and elbows. The jacket is of the brand HIJ, and has as distinguishing characteristic of spots of white paint on the shoulders."

Those spots of white paint had never had any significance for me, but the dry tone of the report, that could have ben written by Martin Bril, made the splashes seem like the Milky Way. Martin Bril, columnist for Het Parool, specialises in those gems that raise crime, or petty criminality to the level of literature. In blank descriptions character traits are magnified, unintended events presented as evidence that the Officer of Justice has overlooked. After the death of Simon Carmiggelt the profession of chronicler was almost extinguished by the demands of the visual culture, but Martin Bril has blown new life into it as a form of contemporary behavioural psychology. That he prefers to describe legal cases is not so surprising. Again a criminal record is the way to preserve our pointless earthly odyssey for posterity.

My Rotterdam tour-guide, Jeroen J., is in his own way also a chronicler. He maps out petty vandalism, appends to it, communicates with those who do it and, by means of his anonymous actions, criticises the creators of the public spaces who work hard to make their environments thug-proof. J. is a self-made behavioural psychologist.

The work is located on a pedestrian island: a triangle formed by the intersection of Broadway and 7th Avenue, between 46th and 45th Streets, in New York City's Times Square. The aural and visual environment is rich and complex. It includes large billboards, moving neon signs, office buildings, hotels, theaters, porno centers and electronic game emporiums. Its population is equally diverse including tourists, theatergoers, commuters, pimps, shoppers, hucksters and office workers. Most people are in motion, passing through the square. The island, as it is the junction of several of the square's pathways, is sometimes crossed by a thousand or more people in an hour.

The work is an invisible unmarked block of sound on the north end of the island. Its sonority, a rich harmonic sound texture resembling the after ring of large bells, is an impossibility within its context. Many who pass through it, however, can dismiss it as an unusual machinery sound from below ground. For those who find and accept the sound's impossibility though, the island becomes a different place, separate, but including its surroundings. These people, having no way of knowing that it has been deliberately made, usually claim the work as a place of their own discovering. Max Neuhaus on Times Square, 1977

Ghost Stories

Based: Los Angeles
Editor/Curator/Designer: Casey McKinney

Ghost Stories Magazine *is the third "magazine" produced and edited by Casey McKinney,*
who is also responsible for Animal Stories Magazine *and* Mall Punk Magazine. *This pub-*
lication started as an art exhibition at Sandroni Rey Gallery in Los Angeles and is described
by McKinney in the following manner: And so we enter Ghost Stories, *something which,*
once again, I know nothing about. It just seems like the logical next step if you consider the
three magazines as a temporal triptych: Animal Stories *representing the primordial past,*
Mall Punk *the incendiary immediate, and* Ghost Stories *the dreaded posthumous, the*
future (which for someone like me, suffering from abulia, is always frightening). So there you
have it. Past, present, future. Kind of like the Bosch painting, The Garden of Delights. *I*
have no idea what is going on, but the very capable and highly talented young artists seem to
get it, and that's all that matters. I would like to thank the formidable artist, three-time mag-
azine contributor and all-around nice person Sue de Beer for inviting me to curate this show.
(You know it's funny, like a geographically reconciliatory rap album, the lineup for this show
is split down the middle, half hailing from Brooklyn, N.Y., the other half from Los Angeles.
Let's hope no one gets shot.)

Poster at right designed by Aaron McDannell, 2001.

49

Hot Rod

Based: Oslo
Editor: Jan Walaker
Designer: Jan Walaker
Email: hotrod@manualdesign.no

Hot Rod *was created in 1998 by Jan Walaker, who has a background in design and photography. The idea was to make a magazine he would be very excited about picking up at the newsstand or from the store. The magazine functions as a space where he can work freely with artists, musicians, designers and writers.*

NOK 69,-
SEK 69,-
DKR 69,-
UK 5 £
US 8 $

art • fashion • music

51

A talk with the dark side

Jan Walaker caught up with the Black Metal scene by talking to Sigurd Wongraven

A fan at Tuska 2000, Helsinki, Finland. Photo: Jan Walaker.

My favourite t-shirt

Photo by

Victor Boullet
Marcel Lelienhof
Rita Mostrøm Larsen / Kristine Jærn Pilgaard
Jamieson Pothecary
Thomas Brun

Victor Boullet, photographer - Hellacopters is a Swedish band, never heard any of their stuff but I love the t-shirt. Another favourite is a Metallica t-shirt. Victor works on a new book and an exhibit this fall at NAF, Oslo.

Index

Based: New York
Publisher: Peter Halley
Associate Publisher: Ariana Speyer
Director of Advertising: Michael Bullock
Editor-in-Chief: Cory Reynolds
Design Director: Stacy Wakefield
Editors: Ariana Speyer and Jesse Pearson
Editor at Large: Steve Lafreniere
Founding Editor: Bob Nickas

Peter Halley and Bob Nickas started index in New York in 1996. Peter, who became the publisher, was already a well-known artist. Bob, who came from a background working as an independent curator and critic, was the first editor.

Peter and Bob started the magazine at a time when the art world was feeling particularly gloomy and politically correct. Their idea was to interview people from different creative fields that big magazines wouldn't talk to—whether they were up-and-coming, already legendary, or important but overlooked. The feeling of the magazine was intimate and chatty. People spoke freely about their lives, their ideas, their work, and, whenever possible, about other more fanciful things.

index's first designer was Laura Genninger. Working out of her apartment, she did all the production, design, and on-site press work by herself. I was the managing editor—meaning that I ran the magazine out of Peter's 26th Street studio, where index is still located. I answered the phones, fixed the machines, and operated the only computer (Bob worked at home on a typewriter for the first few issues, coming in to the studio sporadically). I handled all logistics, proofread, transcribed, and begged stores to carry the magazine. Ariana Speyer soon became the advertising director. She had studied literature, and had no previous experience. At the time, nobody wanted to advertise with an unknown magazine that covered mainly non-celebrities. But Ariana managed to connect us with our original advertising base—the little clothing and design shops that were just beginning to open up around the Lower East Side and Nolita. And that was pretty much it for a while.

index started out oversized, with no text on the cover other than a tiny logo. We printed the magazine on a newspaper press, in black-and-white, using just two old-fashioned fonts throughout the magazine. The type size was large - the interviews looked like film scripts. The design was so pared down and subtle that the magazine was often mistaken for one of two things: a free paper, or an expensive art object. I always thought index felt like a giant zine for off-beat intellectuals. It had a fly-on-the-wall quality too—"This is how John Waters really talks, this is how he really looks, this is how he really thinks."

Despite our humble beginnings and low-tech printing, photographers loved index right from the start. We tried never to crop the pictures that they gave us, and we didn't put text over their images.

Our first cover photographer was Wolfgang Tillmans. His style of portraiture—sweet, natural, sexy, and emotional—really set the tone for the entire magazine. Since then we've assembled an amazing group of photographers who still work with us regularly: Terry Richardson, Juergen Teller, Leeta Harding, Timothy Greenfield-Sanders, Ryan McGinley, Roe Ethridge, Bruce LaBruce, Juliana Sohn, Jessica Craig-Martin, and Mark Borthwick.

Despite our early inexperience, in the first issues of index we did manage to publish interviews with the director, Wes Anderson, whose first movie had not yet been released, the legendary architect and designer, Ettore Sottsass, and the German cult actor, Udo Kier. Over the years, some of my favorite interviews have been with Todd Haynes, David Sedaris, Fischerspooner, Isabella Rossellini, Aphex Twin, Charles Ray, Eileen Myles, Harmony Korine, Bianca Jagger, Takashi Murakami, Rem Koolhaas, Carole Channing, The Melvins, Björk, J.T. LeRoy, and Bless.

By 1999, a number of other magazines had begun to appear that looked like the original index: uncropped, unstyled photos, "casual" interviews, and lots of white space. It was time for us to do something fresh—so in the summer of 2000, we chose Stacy Wakefield to be our new designer. Bob decided to retire, and the editorial roster changed to its current configuration, with Jesse Pearson, Michael Bullock and Steve Lafreniere joining us in major new roles. The magazine opened up a lot more. It became more sophisticated and sexy, more humorous, light-hearted, and accessible.

In 2001, we are launching a book imprint, index books. The first two titles will be small paperback photo books by Ryan McGinley and Bruce LaBruce. We have a second index music CD in the works, and several international photo exhibitions upcoming. A Japanese language edition is in development. And this year we are introducing a website containing the complete archive of our interviews, www.indexmagazine.com. The website isn't as nice as the magazine, but it does bring together a pretty amazing group of people.

index

MAGAZINE   JUNE/JULY 2001

DISPLAY UNTIL JULY 31 $4.50

JT LeRoy   Gavin Brown   Ernesto Esposito   Bless   Paige West
Andy Spade   Rachael Horovitz   Björk   Tom & Sachs
Valerie Steele   Fred Hughes
Steven Mark Klein   Richard Johnson
                     Mariuccia Casadio

index

MAGAZINE SEPT/OCT 98

TERRY RICHARDSON
LILI TAYLOR
CONSTANCE WHITE
YAYOI KUSAMA
WALTER MOSLEY
CAT POWER

WITH CORY REYNOLDS
PHOTOGRAPHED BY LEETA HARDING

JUERGEN TELLER's

PHOTOGRAPHS MAKE ME DESIRE
WHAT'S THERE. THEY ALSO MAKE
ME WONDER WHAT'S JUST OUTSIDE THE PICTURE;
THEY MAKE ME WISH I WERE THERE MYSELF. HIS
WORK IS SEXY, PERCEPTIVE, AND GENTLE. JUERGEN
OFTEN CAPTURES THE UNGUARDED MOMENTS OF THE PEOPLE HE'S PHO-
TOGRAPHING — NO SMALL FEAT, CONSIDERING HE GENERALLY WORKS WITH
TOP MODELS AND CELEBRITIES. WHETHER I'M LOOKING AT A PICTURE OF
BJÖRK AND HER SON IN AN ICELANDIC HOT SPRING, KATE MOSS IN BED ON
THE DAY AFTER HER 25TH BIRTHDAY, KURT COBAIN TUNING HIS GUITAR, OR
O.J. SIMPSON IN AN ANONYMOUS FLORIDA HOTEL ROOM, I ALWAYS FEEL LIKE
I'M JUST ABOUT TO LEARN A SECRET. ¶ JUERGEN'S PHOTOGRAPHS ARE
EVERYWHERE: I-D, PURPLE, W, DAZED & CONFUSED, ALL THE VOGUES. HE'S

town where Adidas was founded, were responsible for deciding how the fabrics were combined.

ARIANA: That must have been interesting.

DESIRÉE: We had to trust them, in terms of how they would put each shoe together. The other day I was talking with the guy who was in charge of the project. Of course the factory workers didn't have the same taste that we did. They were these German women, and they would ask him, "Are you sure this fabric is supposed to go with that one?" Apparently, in one of the bags there wasn't enough fabric to cover the shoe completely, so one woman became super-creative and brought her own fabric from home to make up the difference. It was excellent.

ARIANA: There's so much detail in your work, like the tiny bits of fabric for those sneakers. What do you do to help you escape?

INES: We have the same hobby. We've done aikido for four-and-a-half years. We tried it one hot summer in Berlin and continued from there.

ARIANA: Do you go every week?

DESIRÉE: [laughs] Every day. It's a good break — you don't think about the rest of your life. When you learn a martial art, it's like learning a language. You repeat vocabulary, and sometimes you can't speak because you're missing the right words.

INES: Everybody wears either a white kimono, or a traditional Japanese skirt. The uniform makes everyone equal. You can't tell if a person has an interesting job, or whatever.

ARIANA: So you two met after school?

DESIRÉE: We met at a fashion competition during our studies. But we went to different schools.

ARIANA: You both seem very interested in getting the customer involved with your products.

INES: Absolutely. We're interested in things that are surprising to us as well. That idea was really important for this piece we did called The Set. Just before that we'd done the disposable t-shirts, which we liked a lot. But people were starting to see us as "hot new young designers," and we didn't like that so much.

ARIANA: Why not?

DESIRÉE: People started buying our stuff as the thing to buy that season. So we made The Set, which is a limited edition, and people were really irritated. It showed us who was willing to follow our ideas and who was only interested in the trend of the moment.

ARIANA: So The Set functioned as a weeding-out of your supporters — a social experiment.

INES: That's a good description.

ARIANA: But I don't know what the product is exactly.

DESIRÉE: It's an all-over body accessory, a large piece of fabric on which we placed different things ...

INES: ... like a little piece of leather with a nice pattern imprinted on it.

DESIRÉE: We had a bunch of ideas for a collection that season, so we took the whole lot of them and stuck them on this product. The interesting thing was that quite a few designers bought the piece!

ARIANA: It was like a sketchbook, or a personal scrapbook.

INES: Very much so.

ARIANA: Your approach usually feels so personal. Ines,

what brought you to fashion?

INES: My father is a furrier. We lived in Fürth, near Nuremberg. We inherited the business, which had come down through many generations. So I grew up in the middle of fur coats and all this really nice material which I absolutely loved as a child. All through my childhood I thought I would follow my father, and take over the shop.

ARIANA: Did you spend much time in the fur shop?

INES: Yeah, but when I finished school at seventeen, I knew I didn't want to be a furrier. I was thinking about studying fashion, and I wanted to get as far away as I could. I got accepted at the School for Art and Design, in Hanover. But I got sent back right away because they said I needed to do an internship with a tailor for six months before I could start school.

ARIANA: That's terrible.

INES: I went to work at this haute couture place in Nuremberg, which was a little ridiculous, of course. It was owned by this middle-aged woman with no husband — kind of a witch. All the people who do this old-school haute couture tailoring are weird. She had these fat old rich clients who had no style. I worked such long hours that after only four months I had completed all the requirements. It was like working in prison, but I learned so much. It was incredible.

ARIANA: Desirée, you went to the School of Applied

BLESS NO. 07, LIVING-ROOM CONQUERORS, 1999

JUNE 2001 **INDEX** 49

kara walker
WITH ALEXANDER ALBERRO

ALEXANDER ALBERRO: How did you first come upon your decision to make and exhibit the cut-out silhouettes? Did you initially put them onto canvas?

KARA WALKER: Yes. In Atlanta I was still sort of timidly painting things. Then I began making little oval framed pornographic collages. I would cover up the juicy parts with silhouettes or paperback romance novel heroines. These aren't my favorite artworks but they were almost heading in the direction that I wanted to go. When I left Atlanta, I slowly abandoned oil paint altogether, weaning myself of its obvious seduction and looking for a format that seemed weak.... I suppose I consider the silhouette weak. I wanted to find a format that I could seduce. That seems to me to be in keeping with my mindset. Especially at that time, since I was concentrating a lot on the body of black woman as exotic seductress — purveyor of failed seductions particularly — desire, miscegenation, and historicity and all the complexities of all these things. Eventually, I started cutting silhouettes out of wood with a jigsaw. I first did this with a piece I called Genealogy. I added eyes, lips, tits — that looked like eyes — and blindfolds to some, and placed them on a wall in a manner that alluded to a family tree.

AA: What did your paintings look like?

KW: Well, the paintings were really big. I was trying to make up mythology, and deconstruct it at the same time. I was using classical iconographic things like swans alluding to Leda and the Swan, and hermaphrodites. And I was making hybrid animals as well. But I don't think any of that carried over into my collage work. It was strictly oil painting. Large oil painting, with thick and juicy brushwork.

AA: So there was quite a transformation in your work after you left Atlanta.

KW: Oh, yeah, it was a conscious change. I was determined to be better; to make work that would actually stimulate others, and not just myself. I figured that if I succeeded in one radical transformation, then I could do anything. In a way, a lot of this has to do with my leaving the South. In Atlanta, I was very consciously trying to stay away from race issues. There it was hard to really

see these issues since the culture is so extremely black and white. I mean, there are black artists doing work that deals with race issues in Atlanta, but I thought it all looked the same. I didn't want to be a part of that.

AA: Why the silhouettes, then?

KW: Somewhere along the way I, like many other people, became interested in kitschy items such as Sam Keane's big-eyed children that you find on prints everywhere. So the silhouette images were popping up here and there but I wasn't really thinking of them as anything other than kitsch. I hadn't really investigated them as having a fairly rich history. I was thinking about blackness, and minstrelsy, and the kind of positions that I was putting myself in at home in Atlanta. I mean, I was testing the ground to see what kind of a person I was perceived as, or what kind of a person I was thinking of myself as. I mean, I saw myself as someone who was locked in histories, as a nebulous, shadowy character from a romance novel, but not a novel that anyone ever remembered.

AA: What did you see in the kitsch object that intrigued you enough to take it up in your work? What was it that attracted you to the Sam Keane objects and motifs?

KW: I think I liked the fact that they were just awful. I mean, I thought that if it's ineffective to make paintings of things that one loves and finds meaningful, then what happens when one makes pictures of things that one would never want to see a picture of? So I tried that for a little while. The big-eyed girl went over pretty well but it wasn't a lasting project. But the silhouette children kept popping up. Initially just little sketches and tiny paintings here and there, but developed into something much more prevalent. In fact, they took on greater importance when I began thinking about minstrelsy and putting on the Other person and interracial desire — when I attempted to see from the other person's point of view: from the point of view of the white male master from American history. The silhouette says a lot with very little information, but that's also what the stereotype does. So I saw the

24 index

index 25

Kit & Caboodle

Based: New York
Editors: Kevin Hatt, Simone Colina & Phil Bicker

Kit and Caboodle *is an occasionally published photography magazine. Known as a small* publication (pocketsize) Kit and Caboodle *is a very intimate photography experience.*

Kevin Hatt, a photographer himself, publishes this magazine with Simone Colina, fashion stylist (Revlon, Versace, Levis, GAP) and art director Phil Bicker (Face, International Vogue Homme, Blackbook). Through a network of photographers from NY, London, Paris, Vancouver work is submitted of each photographers own liking. The compilation results in an opinion of photography of the time.

KIT & CABOODLE

31

60

22   23

Lab

Based: London
Editor: Pavlova
Art Directors: Astrid Stavro and Joana Ramos-Pinto
Fashion Editor: Laia Farran
Email: lab@associate.co.uk

Lab *magazine is a laboratory of visual experimentation. It was born in September 2000 with the aim to create a new kind of space for artists to present their work and express their creativity, and to design a network through which people working in different disciplines could easily access new information and each other. The main concept behind* Lab *is to promote new unestablished artists, to serve as a launch-pad for young creatives in the graphic design, photography, fashion and music industries. A typical issue features interviews, articles and presentations covering a wide range of topics and disciplines, built around a loose theme that serves to create a link between subjects and collaborators. The art direction of* Lab *reflects the spirit of the magazine by constantly changing and experimenting with the layout, the typefaces and the grid. In* Lab *nothing is permanent. Even the collaborators change from one issue to the next. We don't build up catalogues of names but rather pass them on. That is what* Lab *is here for: to hunt, to discover, to share the passion and then move on.*

SPRING 2001
ISSUE 01 > £4.20

9 771473 337009

0 1>

ARTMIKS

A good design starts with a good concept. It sounds like stating the obvious, but in practice this important first step is all too often skipped. The designers of the Dutch graphic design agency Artmiks (image builders), develop strong and well thought-out concepts for every specific client or assignment, using their various backgrounds (web and graphic design, illustration, animation, sound-editing, programming, etc.), in the actual design, we stay away from standard solutions and established lines. For internet assignments, we always search for a unique navigation, suitable sound and images and a surprising layout. Hugo Kalf and Marco de Sider founded Artmiks (image builders) in 1995. At first, the assignments were mostly in graphic design. Last year, after launching our own project hyperlink www.pureid.af, web design got more and more important. The goal of the Pure campaign is to attract the sort of clients we want to work for, by showing our conceptual way of working, which so far, has reached quite well. Clients who now approach Artmiks, know that they're not going to leave with the usual pages with buttons and navigation bar. This summer, the successor to Puree (working title: P3) will be launched. Lab magazine kindly gave us the opportunity to show examples of our work on these pages. But since interactivity is a difficult thing to show in print, we prefer to invite you to visit www.artmiks.af, which has links to all our recent projects. And as a special Lab bonus: www.artmiks.nl/kindergarten

PEACE
CONVOY

_OPIE

JULIAN OPIE'S WORK HAS BEEN DESCRIBED AS ONE OF COOL UNDER-STATEMENT. USING COMPUTERS TO EXPLORE THE ILLUSION OF SPACE AND VISUAL LANGUAGE, RATHER LIKE EARLY RENAISSANCE PAINTERS ENGAGED IN THEIR SEARCH FOR PERSPECTIVE, OPIE'S SUCCESS LIES BEHIND HIS CONSTANT DECODING OF MODERN LIFE USING A NUMBER OF SYSTEMS THAT HAVE BECOME ROOTED IN SOCIETY AND TRANSGRESSING THEIR NATURAL HABITAT. LANGUAGES JUXTAPOSED TO CREATE NEW MESSAGES.

Lab Editor Astrid Stavro and I arrive at the studio on time to find Julian buried in paperwork. He is very welcoming and promptly offers us a cup of coffee. The studio is a big space full of rolls of paper, stacks of magazines and canvases leaning against the wall. I follow him into the living area to the kitchen, and find myself faced with a black rabbit – Flopsy – who stares at me questioningly. In that charmingly insolent way that only children and animals can get away with. Soon she looses interest and hops off. I explain that our current issue is based on the theme 'Kindergarten', and how we thought Playmobil resembled his portraits...

Is there a conscious connection there? Not directly with Playmobil. I didn't think I was that aware of Playmobil when I started dealing with that kind of imagery. Playmobil must be 1960's. I grew up with Scalextric and Tin-Tin. A lot of people have also mentioned Southpark because of the landscape, but I wasn't aware of it. I

think that there is a background, a history of cartoon imagery that you can take back to Japanese prints - 18th and 19th century Japanese wood-block prints, Re Hokusai - where everything is flattened out, but also quite three-dimensional. In European culture you can take it back to some of the earliest cartoons, which were religious ones in the Renaissance. For example, they told the story of Saint John and there would be a series of panels, by people like Giotto... those were the sort of images I was looking at, images that were simple and readable, and somehow outside of a strictly art reading. By using something that has a childlike or a cartoonish quality I think you kind of duck out from something looking too much like art and I have always tried to find other languages, visual languages, other than one which refers to art. Although I use that one too, for example, the picture behind you looks like a reclining nude, she is in a position which is a classical painting type of reclining nude position, but the way she is drawn

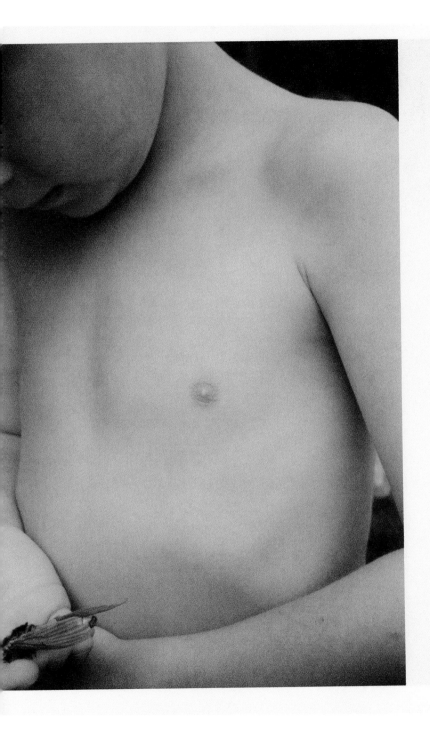

10 – Hugo, Marco, Michael, Vincent, Melissa, Barbara, Roberta, Fleur, Evangelos, Andreas and dog Gepp, illustrated by Fleur.

3 LOST ANIMALS, 2001
1994, ALUMINIUM STEEL

...is more like a lavatory sign which is another visual language...
What I do is to mix all these languages together.
That is what makes it interesting. It is mixing languages that has always been the core of my work, it is mixing languages and then mixing them in an unusual way; perhaps I will mix a road sign with a very personal image of my girlfriend, so on the one hand you may have one language which is very formal, authoritative and on the other hand you have one that is very intimate. A childlike quality is often very useful, because it is attractive. It is appealing, it is kind of innocent and, like a lot of the Japanese imagery you see around, if you mix that with something that is a bit more sophisticated, a bit more stylish, possibly a bit more dangerous or worldly, you get a tension, which is exciting. About the languages... I think the way that children learn is a visual process about looking and touching things – that is how we build up our sense of the world which we then take for granted.

It is a learnt process. That is perhaps what I am trying to focus on and take a few steps back down the level of learning, and just say: "OK, here is a car, and what does it do against this? OK, so it becomes the road..." to build up slowly that kind of simple imagery.

Encoding and decoding is central to Opie's work. From the obvious to the smallest detail. An example of this is Opie's exhibition in 1996 where the 'catalogue' is a thick, children-style book in thick card – yet another level of language.
The catalogue looks like a kid's book. Yes, this one here was the last catalogue I did for the exhibition we held at Lisson Gallery. It is designed to look more like a freebie you get for bad furniture, and this one – handing over a brochure – is designed to look more like a Women's magazine.
Do you have a favourite toy? Then or now? Either...To be honest if it is a toy now, it is Tomb Raider. I find it fascinating visually and

List

Based: New York
Publishers: Michael Donahue, Serge Becker and CAN Resources
Editors-in-Chief: Lisa Ano and Serge Becker
Editorial Assistant: Amani Vance
Design/Production Assistants: Steven Baillie and Danae Grandison
Photo Research Assistant: Shira Bocar
Email: info@listmag.com
www.listmag.com

List
00 a periodical
01 entirely in list format
02 on paper
03 on screen
04 by contributors in the know
05 for people who want to know
06 and not afraid to ask
07 random thoughts
08 sly observations
09 candid opinions
10 obsessive musings
11 notes from the underground
12 personal records
13 about art
14 about commerce
15 about process
16 about fashion
17 about fucking
18 about words
19 about music
20 about politics
21 about shopping
22 about nothing
23 about us
24 easy to read
25 informative
26 uncut
27 irreverent
28 smart
29 visual
30 condensed
31 always changing
32 connect the dots
33 start the dialogue

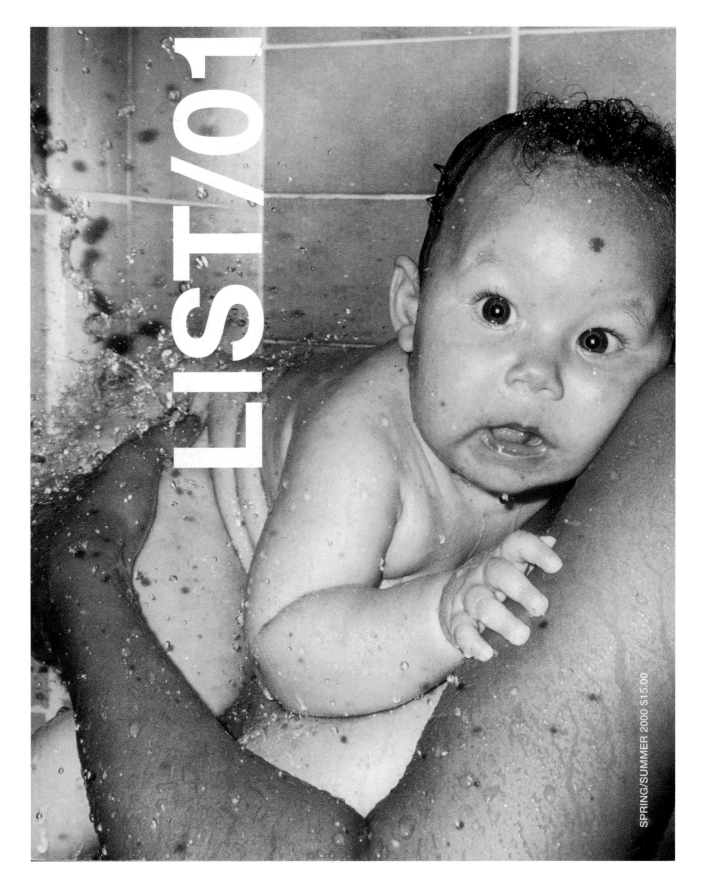

LIST/01

SPRING/SUMMER 2000 $15.00

Sigfried and Roy
Jocelyn Wildenstein
Donatella Versace
Billie Jean King

TOP NEWSPAPERS BY CIRCULATION

UNITED STATES - DAILY

NEWSPAPER	DAILY CIRCULATION
1. New York (NY) *Wall Street Journal*	1,746,450
2. Arlington (VA) *USA Today*	1,653,428
3. Los Angeles (CA) *Times*	1,067,540
4. New York (NY) *Times*	1,066,658
5. Washington (DC) *Post*	759,122
6. New York (NY) *Daily News*	723,143
7. Chicago (IL) *Tribune*	673,508
8. Long Island (NY) *Newsday*	578,444
9. Houston (TX) *Chronicle*	550,763
10. Chicago (IL) *Sun-Times*	485,666
11. Dallas (TX) *Morning News*	479,863
12. San Francisco (CA) *Chronicle*	475,324
13. Boston (MA) *Globe*	470,825
14. New York (NY) *Post*	437,467
15. Phoenix (AZ) *Arizona Republic*	435,330
16. Philadelphia (PA) *Inquirer*	428,895
17. Newark (NJ) *Star-Ledger*	407,026
18. Cleveland (OH) *Main Dealer*	382,933
19. Detroit (MI) *Free Press*	378,256
20. San Diego (CA) *Union-Tribune*	378,112

www.mediainfo.com, as of September 30, 1999

PLAYLIST

A.P.C., NYC
1. A.P.C. Track 1
2. Lili Boniche Dub
3. Havana Mood
4. Dub Conference - Hiroshi Fujiwara
5. Snatch - Howie B
6. Radiohead
7. Leslie Winer
8. Trojans Rocksteady (boxset)
9. Home with the Groovebox
10. Chant Down Babylon - Bob Marley

KCRW - LOS ANGELES DJ PICKS (10 x 5) JUNE 2000

NIC HARCOURT: Morning Becomes Eclectic

ARTIST	ALBUM	LABEL
John Lennon	Imagine (remixed/remastered)	Capitol
Travis	The Man Who	Epic
Jeff Buckley	Mystery White Boy	Columbia
Elliot Smith	Figure 8	DreamWorks
Various Artists	More Old School vs. New School	Jive/Electro
PJ Olsson	Words for Living	Columbia C2
Rhinocerose	Installation Sonore	V2
Iarla O Lionaird	I Could Reach the Sky	RealWorld
XTC	Wasp Star	TVT
Roy Budd	Get Carter (reissue)	Castle Music America

JASON BENTLEY: Metropolis

ARTIST	ALBUM	LABEL
Femi Kuti	Shoki Remixed	Nuphonic
Tosca	Suzuki	G-Stone
LTJ Bukem	Journey Inwards	Kinetic
Primal Scream	Most Wanted single	Vulture
Running	Xtrmntr	Creation
MJ Cole	Sincere single	Talkin' Loud
Various Artists	Human Traffic soundtrack	London
Chemical Brothers	Music : Response single remixes	Astralwerks
Various Artists	More Old School vs. New School	Jive/Electro
Dimitri from Paris	A Night at the Playboy Mansion	Astralwerks

TOM SCHNABEL: Café LA

ARTIST	ALBUM	LABEL
Joni Mitchell	Both Sides Now	Reprise
Amel Larrieux	Infinite Possibilities	Epic
Rick Margitza	Heart of Heart	Palmetto
Various Artists	No Categories Vol. 3	Ubiquity
Nass Marrakech	Sabil'a Salaam	Alula
Bebel Gilberto	Tanto Tempo	Six Degrees
Hesperion XXI	Diaspora Sefardi	Aliavox
Various Artists	Putumayo presents Republica Dominicana	Putumayo
Anabela	Origens	Movieplay Portuguesa
J.S. Bach	Sonatas & Partitas; Hopkinson Smith, Lute	Astree

GARTH TRINIDAD: Chocolate City

ARTIST	ALBUM	LABEL
Various Artists	Prime Cuts Vol.1	Delicious Vinyl
Azymuth	Pieces of Ipanema	Far Out
Common	Like Water for Chocolate	MCA
Camille Yarbrough	The Iron Pot Cooker	Vanguard
Bossa Tres	Jazz	Yellow Productions
Tekg	Simply	SSR
Glenn Underground	Lounge Excursions	Guidance
Donald Byrd	Stepping into Tomorrow	Blue Note
Various Artists	Eargasms Vol.1	Ozone Music
Bebel Gilberto	Tanto Tempo	6 Degrees

LIZA RICHARDSON: The Drop

ARTIST	ALBUM	LABEL
Various Artists	Nude Dimensions Vol. 2	Naked Music Recordings
Moloko	Time Is Now	Echo
Various Artists	Goodvibe Recordings 2000	Goodvibe/Atomic Pop
Zuco 103	Outro Lado	Six Degrees
Jephte Guillaume	Priye-A (The Prayer)	Chrysalis/France
George Benson	El Barrio	GRP
Various Artists	Idjut Boys Saturday Night Live	Nuphonic
Various Artists	The Voices of Urban Renewal	Guida
Full Intention	Everybody Loves the Sunshine	Legato Records

APOTHIA at Fred Segal, LA
1. On How Life Is - Macy Gray
2. Chant Down Babylon - Bob Marley
3. Voodoo - D'Angelo
4. Rave Un 2 the Joy Fantastic - Prince
5. Mary - Mary J Blige
6. Play - Moby
7. Black Diamond - Angie Stone
8. My Dream - Yvette Michel
9. Jive Dance Party Hits
10. New Sound of Venezuelan - Los Amigos Invisible Gozadera

CANTEEN, NYC
1. Jet Society - 18th Street Lounge
2. Caliente - Bossa Brava
3. Best of - Stan Getz
4. James Hardway
5. Roots of Acid Jazz - Cal Tjader
6. Mr Electric Triangle - Bossa Nova
7. Remember Me - Blue Boy
8. Midnight Calling - Mark Farina
9. Honey - Suzuki
10. Sixth Sense- United Future Organization

DDC Lab, NYC
1. Splinter - Sneaker Pimps
2. All Hands on the Bad One - Sleater-Kinney
3. WXBD- Buffalo Daughter
4. Singles Collection - David Bowie
5. Cobra & Phases Group Play Voltage in the Miky Night - Stereolab
6. Is This Desire? - PJ Harvey
7. Salt Peter Remixed - Ruby
8. Alel Empire + The Destroyer
9. 1000 Fires - Traci Lords
10. This Is Hardcore - Pulp

FILTH MART, NYC
1. AC/DC
2. Black Sabbath
3. David Bowie
4. Van Halen w/David Lee Roth only!
5. The Unband
6. Lynard Skynard
7. Motley Crue
8. Guns N' Roses
9. The Voluptuous Horror of Karen Black
10. Rolling Stones

H&M, NYC
1. Destiny's Child
2. Jennifer Lopez
3. Mariah Carey
4. Satana
5. Blessed Union of Souls
6. Macy Gray
7. Filter
8. Celine Dion
9. Lenny Kravitz
10. Geri Halliwell

K-MART, NYC
1. Beth - Kiss
2. Here Comes the Sun - The Beatles
3. I Still Believe - Mariah Carey
4. Love Song - The Cure
5. Please Don't Tell Her - Big Head Todd & the Monsters
6. Slide - Goo Goo Dolls
7. Three Marlenas - The Wallflowers
8. Time of Your Life - Green Day
9. Together Again - Janet Jackson
10. We've Got Tonight - Bob Seger

JetBlue Airlines
1. I Got a Right to Sing the Blues - Lena Horne
2. Blue Velvet - Bobby Vinton
3. Have You Ever Had It Blue? - Style Council
4. Joy and Blues- Ziggy Marley
5. Perfect Blue - Lloyd Cole & the Commotions
6. Running Blue - Roz Scaggs
7. Sky Blue and Blade - Jackson Browne
8. Lady Blue - George Benson
9. It's All Over Now Baby Blue - Van Morrison
10. Hey Blue - Tony Rich Project

MOSS, NYC
1. Dance Rajah Dance - Vijaya Anand
2. Poupee de Son - France Gall
3. Jackie Girl - Louis Philippe
4. Fairytales & Fantasies - Lee Hazelwood/Nancy Sinatra
5. Walking On Thin Ice - Yoko Ono
6. The Pleasure Principle - Gary Numan
7. Xanadu - Olivia Newton-John
8. Music for Imaginary Films - Arling & Cameron
9. (Bootleg) - Fisherspooner
10. Rhythm Nation - Janet Jackson

PASTIS, NYC
1. Caminando - Tonny Tun Tun
2. Instant Soul - The Legendary King Curtis
3. Tout Eddy - Eddy Mitchell
4. Blue Valentine - Tom Waits
5. Pintame - Elvis Crespo
6. Dynamite - Tommy McCook
7. Look Out - Stanley Turrentine
8. Les Rita Mitsouko
9. Grandes Exitos - Tito Rodriguez
10. Sugar's Boogaloo - Sugarman Three

SUPREME, NYC
1. Supreme Clientele - Ghostface Killah
2. 400 Degreez - Juvenile
3. Lets Get Free - Dead Prez
4. Inna Heights - Buju Banton
5. Live at the Village Vanguard- John Coltrane
6. All Time Greatest Hits - James Brown
7. (last 3 CD's) - Outkast
8. 2001 Instrumental - Dr. Dre
9. War Report - Capone -N- Noreaga
10. Life After Death - Notorious B.I.G.

VIRGIN ATLANTIC AIRLINES
"Soul Plane Station"
1. Turn Your Lights Down Low - remix Bob Marley & Lauryn Hill
2. I Try (JayDee remix) - Macy Gray
3. Makeda (DJ Spinna & Ticklah remix) - Les Nubians
4. Dreaming of Loving You - David's Daughters
5. Still Believe (Dodge Soul Faith mix) - Shola Ama
6. 'Bout it (So SoDef remix) - Jesse Powell
7. What Y'all Want - Eve
8. Will 2K - Will Smith
9. Frenemy - Me-One
10. Role Model - Eminem
11. What You Want - The Roots feat. Jaguar
12. Angel in Disguise - Brandy
13. Battle - Wookie featuring Laine
14. Yesterday - Katt
15. Space Rider - Shaun Escoffery
16. Sweeter Love - Blue 6
17. Rescue Me - Sunkids featuring Chance
18. I Shall Not be Moved - Underground Ministries
19. Down On Me - Wookie
20. What's Going On? - Soul II Soul

ZAO, NYC
1. Paid in Full: The Platinum Edition - Erik B. and Rakim
2. Rhythm & Stealth - Leftfield
3. gB (sampler)
4. ut Flowers - Chomeric Mosquito
5. We'll Never Stop Living This Ways-Westbam
6. The Beat Assassinated - DJ Cam
7. Roxbox - Zoa
8. Xanadu Elvis/Lost in Space - Kool Keith
9. H_2O - Liquid Groove
10. DJ Kicks - Thievery Corporation

NY TAXI/Raza Ahmad #JP1
Nusrat Fateh Ali Khan (vol. 1-5) in concert in Paris
Lata Mangeshkar
The Golden Voice of Mukesh
103.5 FM
Ricky Martin "Livin' la Vida Loca"
Celine Dion "My Heart Will Go On" from Titanic
Michael Jackson
101.9 FM
92.3 FM
Howard Stern
Cab Message: "This is Judge Judy Sheindlin and Judge Jerry Sheindlin. Don't be stupid, do the right thing, BUCKLE UP! It's Judge Judy and Judge Jerry. We don't want to see you in court so don't forget to take your belongings and get a receipt from your driver. You're in New York City, the millennium capital of the world!"

trivia**LIST**

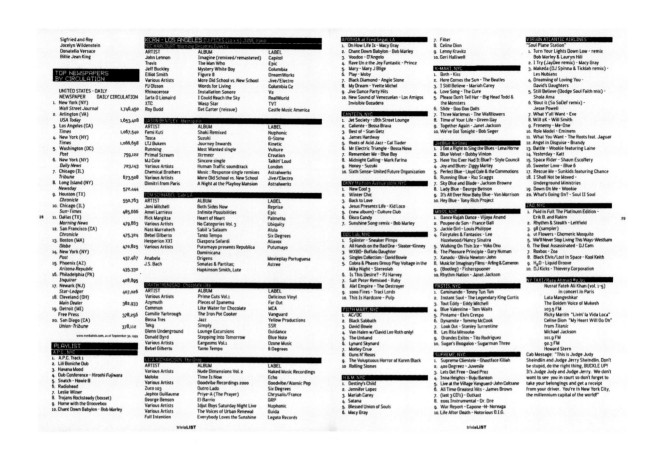

vocabulary**LIST**

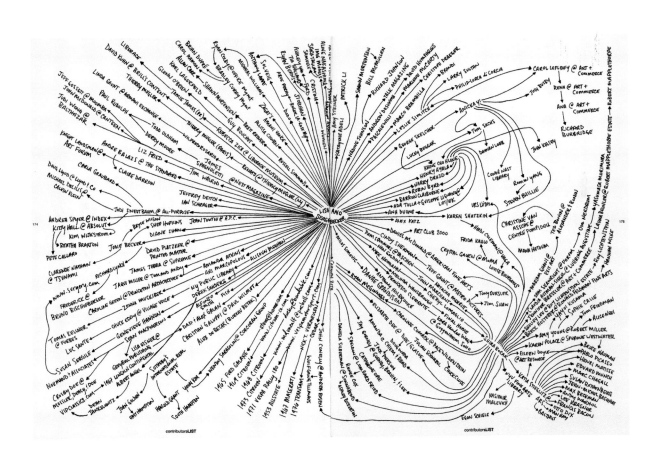

Mall Punk

Based: Los Angeles
Editor: Casey McKinney
Designer: Casey McKinney

Mall Punk *was originally intended to be a kind of sappy, nostalgic eulogy to a certain period of life, while simultaneously serving as an aggressive critique of consumer culture and the apparent futility of rebellion in an age of hyper-commodification (yes, I was freshly, abashedly, brimming with school damage at that point). But happily the idea soon morphed as contributors inserted their own meaning into the concept, and it blossomed into the beautiful and gory thing that it is.*

Mall Punk Magazine

Issue 1   Fall 2000 $8 US

Brent Adams, Ben Arnold, Alissa Bennett, Chris Bilheimer, Jesse Bransford, Todd Cole, Dennis Cooper, Sue De Beer, Trinie Dalton, Bret Easton Ellis, Jason Forrest, Helen Garber, Mark Gonzales, Amanda Greene, Matthew Greene, Eric Heist, Simon Henwood, Chris Johanson, J.T. LeRoy (A.K.A. Terminator), Casey McKinney, Matt Miller, Laura Parnes, Brian Pera, Raymond Pettibon, Henrik Plenge-Jakobson, Frances Stark, Ed Templeton, Banks Violette, Benjamin Weissman, Tobin Yelland

Dear Reader, Damien Echols,

by Frances Stark

Dear Reader, Damien Echols,

Ever since I saw the documentary about your case I have often thought about writing you a letter. I am not in the habit of writing letters to death row inmates, although I have in the past written a handful of fan letters to various musicians most of which I shamelessly submitted for publication in places where the original addressee would not be looking. It seems I'm at it again, but not exactly and let me explain. I'm not going to publish this letter I'm just going to read it in public. There are sooo many reasons for this and I probably won't be able to get to them all, but I guess I should just start explaining what this letter is all about. First of all, you've probably already noticed that in addition to the letter I've sent you a book, "A Reader" by Raymond Pettibon. I'm really crossing my fingers that the book passes whatever twisted and irrational guidelines your prison has in operation. I heard you were not allowed to receive a book by Elaine Pagels, who wrote the Gnostic Gospels. I'm wondering if the term "Scholarly text" means anything to those guys in charge out there in Arkansas. Anyway I bring that up because I am worried a bit that you won't have received The Pettibon Reader because it includes a portion of Charles Manson's testimony. I'm assuming if they were to browse the table of contents they would pass right over John Ruskin, George Santayana, and Marcel Proust and see Manson's name and then chuck the book in the trash or whatever they do with unfit material. I was hoping they might notice it was published by an art museum, which just goes to show that I am quick to depend on the legitimizing capacity of an art institution. I guess you could say Shakespeare is somewhat of an art institution and his legitimizing capacity didn't seem to help you in the least in court. In fact because you copied some of Shakespeare's words into your own handwriting, and those words were complicated and referred to death, your jury seemed to think you were capable of murder. It's sad when straight-up ignoramuses can't understand the notion of art, because you can't even use the "it's art" defense on them. There's this story in the Reader by this writer Bernard Welt, by the time I read his story I was already thinking of sending you the book. It's called "A Reply to My Critics" and it's written from the point of view of an

artist who has been convicted of a brutal killing. I am certain that you will enjoy this piece of writing. I was also worried though, again imagining the prison personnel picking up the book and opening to that story seeing something about decapitation and just being grossed out, or pretending to be, and not understanding the context. Speaking of context let me finally get back to the writing of this letter, the sending of the Reader, and the reading of the letter about the Reader. The artist, Raymond Pettibon, is having an exhibition at the Museum of Contemporary Art in Los Angeles where I live. I have been invited to do a reading at the museum with several other writers and artists in honor of Raymond Pettibon. Raymond is an artist I love and an artist whose work I was looking at on record covers before I ever really knew anything about what you can find in art museums. The first thing I saw was this drawing on the cover of Black Flag's Jealous Again. At age 14, it both disturbed and mesmerized me: some sort of unsympathetically rendered cheerleaders had shot an unsympathetic jock in the head…it was a conundrum somehow. Just the year prior I was a cheerleader, which nobody ever believes, but now, a wiser 14 year old with some punk records, I had discovered a different approach to living. Anyway, I really should concentrate on the present. I wanted to tell you about this event and how it applies to you. This writer Benjamin Weissman, invited me to read along with some other people, one of which is Dennis Cooper. These two guys, writers in whom you might take a special interest, were the ones responsible, really, for me finding out about you. Somehow Benjamin had the HBO movie on tape before it was ever released and he loaned it to Dennis. Dennis and I watched it together and we were both totally impressed with you, the way you stood up to the cops on the witness stand and all that. Well the movie's old news and I'm sure you're sick of hearing about it, even so, it is the reason you know nothing about the people who know a lot about you. I was going to tell you all about me, but then I thought I should give you this book, and that's enough. I am sure you will really enjoy the drawings of Raymond's and all the texts he has culled together. There is also an essay in the back by this guy named Hamza Walker; it's called don't throw out the shaman with the bath water or something like that, which is a historical look at Raymond's work and why he's so attached to "late six-

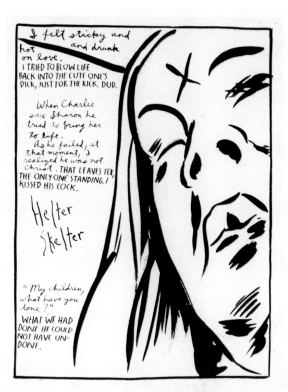

No Title (I felt sticky). 1988. Pen and ink on paper.
14.5 x 11.5. Courtesy of Regen Projects, L.A.

Raymond Pettibon

Jason Forrest
Bike Terrorists, 1998. Color print on Plexiglass.
48 x 60. Courtesy of the artist.

McSweeney's

Based: New York
Copy Editor: Chris Gage
Managing Editor: Erika Kawalek
McSweeney's President: Sarah Min
Editor/Designer: Dave Eggers
www.mcsweeneys.net

McSweeney's *is an extremely self-reflexive magazine about everything and nothing. While editor/founder Dave Eggers maintains that the magazine does not have an editorial statement, their web site tells us that "*McSweeney's *is a quarterly publication. Its issues are on average 280 pages, and are perfect-bound. The contents of* McSweeney's *include fiction, nonfiction, drawings of hairy people and very little poetry."*

TIMOTHY

MᶜSWEENEY

IS STARING LIKE THAT WHY DOES HE KEEP STARING?

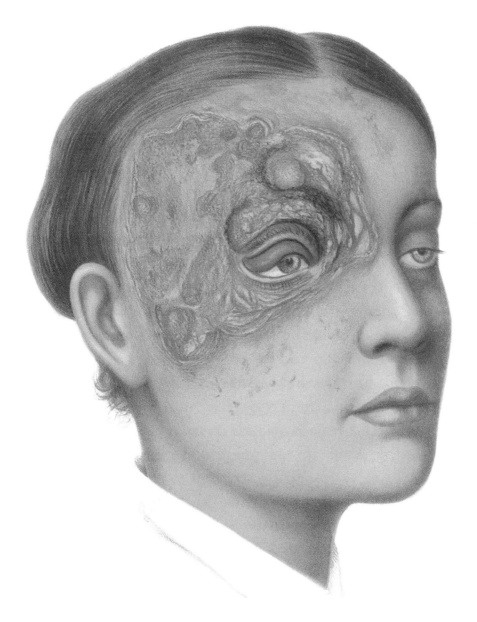

ISSUE NO. 5

VERY LATE SUMMER, 2000

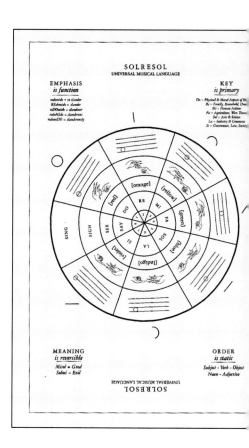

THE
STRANGE *and* EPIC *and* TRAGIC
TRAJECTORY *of*

SOLRESOL, THE UNIVERSAL MUSICAL LANGUAGE
AND OF ITS CREATOR, MONSIEUR SUDRE.

by PAUL COLLINS

IMAGINE FOR A MOMENT a universal language: translatable to color, melody, writing, touch, hand signals, and endless strings of numbers. Imagine now that this language was taught from birth to be second nature to every speaker, regardless of their first language. The world would become saturated with hidden meanings. Music would be transformed, with every instrument in the orchestra at a opera engaged in simultaneous dialogue: cellos darkly muttering melancholy comments about the protagonist while the French horns wander aloud about the unlikely plot, and oboes informing the audience of the baked goods available at the concession stand. People could, through hand signals, hold silent conversation with each other across crowded spaces, allowing them to silently critique the contralto during an opera performance.

The rise and fall of voice in a conversation could carry a subtext, with the internal melody of speech expressing an entirely opposite or hidden sentiment. Skilled speakers could employ a sort of musical counterpoint to their words, with meanings running in parallel, in contrast, and commenting parenthetically upon their own words even as they uttered them.

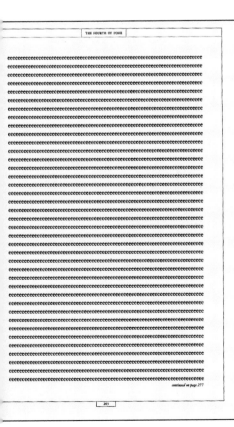

continued on page 277

Merge

Based: Stockholm
Editors-in-Chief: Bo Madestrand and Håkan Nilsson
Editors: Tor Lindstrand and Devin Wilson
UK Editor: Bradly Quinn
US Editor: Stephan Pasher
Art Director: Charlotte Sunna
Designers: Kristina Jonsson and Robert Ahlborg

Merge *is a quarterly international cultural magazine covering a wide range of topics. Art, music, architecture, design, film, philosophy—if we like it, we print it. While the average magazine attempts to explain Everything about Something, our motto is: Anything about Anything. Each issue should reflect our own broad interests as well as those of the writers we work with.*

merge **0**

SOUND THOUGHT IMAGE

Dennis Rodman

Rachel Whiteread

Spencer Finch

Ernst Jünger

KLF

United States $ 7.50   merge #0 1998
Great Britain £ 4.50   ISSN 1402-6570
Sweden 60 SEK

merge #2
MAGAZINE
FALL 98

FREE CD
72 MINUTES OF MUSIC
BARRY ADAMSON, MOUSE ON MARS
NÅID, NATNOS, AND MORE

INDIA
A STATE OF MIND

MOUSE ON MARS
THOSE ALIEN RODENTS

MARADONA
SAINT OR SINNER?

SURVIVAL OF THE FATTEST
FACT OR FICTION?

HEGEL
SOUNDS THE IDEAL

RAUSCHENBERG
THE MUDDY WATERS OF ART

BERLIN
FROM METROPOLIS TO SUBTROPOLIS

United States $7   Sweden 70 SEK   Merge #2 1998
Great Britain £5.10   Canada $10   ISSN 1433-4508
                        France Fr 40   UPC 74251-74768-83

merge #3
SOUND THOUGHT IMAGE
WINTER 98

LOVE

GEEK CHIC
HOW NERDS STOLE THE IDEA OF FASHION

AL GREEN
THE GREATEST SOUL SINGER OF ALL TIME

LEIF ELGGREN
TALKS TO DEAD QUEENS AND WRITES TO CINDY CRAWFORD

FROM BEIRUT WITH LOVE
SHALL WE EAT NOW OR WAIT FOR THE CEASE-FIRE?

SQUAREPUSHER
COMPLEX BREAKNECK BREAKBEATS

With contributions by **Douglas Coupland** and **Slavoj Zizek**

Merge #3 1998
ISSN 1433-4508
UPC 73361-94746-84
Sweden 50 SEK
Canada $7
France Fr 40
United States $5
Great Britain £6

LIFE DURING WARTIME

EVEN WHEN THERE IS A WAR RAGING, LIFE MUST GO ON. DURING THE ISRAELI SIEGE OF BEIRUT, PEOPLE STILL TRIED TO CONDUCT BUSINESS AS USUAL, TO EAT, PARTY, PLAY TENNIS AND MAKE LOVE. KRISTINA RIEGERT RECAPTURES THE SPIRIT OF A CITY WHICH JUST WOULDN'T GIVE UP.

Top: Postcard of Beirut's legendary green line, the centre of town, before 1974.
Bottom: Beirut's green line in 1993. Modern ruins turned tourist trap. Postcard salesmen under umbrellas sell images like the one above.

There are scores of books on the subject of siege from the medieval period up until the late 18th century, but trying to find information about modern siege is like looking for a needle in a haystack. According to the website "Siege Warfare," siege went out of fashion in the 16th century with the introduction of gunpowder, which rendered the defence of castles obsolete. But while laying siege to castles may have gone out of style, sieges of cities continue, almost as an afterthought, within the wider context of contemporary warfare. In the 20th century alone, we have the great sieges of the Second World War, the Viet Cong's sieges of US encampments during the Vietnam War, the Israeli siege of Beirut in 1982, not to mention the sieges of Sarajevo, Mostar and Dubrovnik in the 1990s.

Aside from the military aspects of siege warfare there is an important psychological aspect: siege is per definition directed at both civilians and military. The medieval notion of siege is quite simplistic and is still very much applicable today. The attacker surrounds the castle, city, or camp. All supplies are prevented from going in, and all outgoing traffic is controlled by the attacker. Then the idea is simply to wait for the defenders to become so demoralised from hunger, rats and lack of provisions that they are forced into submission. During this time, anywhere from months to years, the castle (or city, as it were) is constantly bombarded with whatever the attackers can come across.

One tactic used in the medieval period was to catapult the heads of slain enemies over the castle walls to spread terror among the populace. Today's carpet bombing tactics are hardly less "barbaric."

While basic siege tactics may be the same, no two sieges are alike. Maybe this has to do with the fact that no two cities are alike, a city's Geist is the result of its history, its people and its circumstances. Thus, the character of the Israeli siege of Beirut in the summer of 1982 and the reactions of its inhabitants were unique. At the time of the siege, Beirut was de facto a divided city where the so-called green line separated East and West Beirut. This was the result of a civil war which had been going on intermittently since 1975 and which continued some nine years after the Israeli invasion. The mainly Christian Eastern half of the city was thus not subjected to the Israeli siege, whereas the Western half was basically bottled up from 30 June to 18 August 1982.

The ongoing civil war in Lebanon meant that the people of Beirut were quite used to gunfire breaking out at any time of the day or night. One common impression visitors had during this period was how quickly the streets would spring to life after these incidents. When shelling and sniping broke out, shops would close, people would go into hiding, but less than an hour after the fighting died down

people would be back on the streets selling their wares and going about their business. This lifestyle meant that when a Beiruti asked, "How is it outside?" They would not be referring to the weather, but whether there was fighting going on in the neighbourhood. There were thus many ways to die in Beirut – long before the Israelis came.

FUN, SUN, SHOPPING... AND WAR

Despite the long years of civil strife, Beirutis have never forgotten what it was like to be the world-famous capital of fun, sun and shopping. In the sixties, Beirut was the banking capital of the Arab world. People flocked to the "Switzerland" of the Middle East, not only because of its business opportunities, but because there were great casinos, huge luxury hotels and wonderful beaches. This was a time when the mix of some 17 different Christian, Muslim and Druze religions seemed to enhance the perception of Beirut as a liberal and pluralistic city, a place where Orient could meet Occident and get along with each other. When the PLO moved to Beirut in 1970, they found a mecca of intellectual stimuli, potential allies to their cause, not to mention the night life. People did their own thing in Beirut. But doing their own thing led to the formation of factional and political militias who established their own zones throughout the city. Doing their own thing also led to the PLO's "state within a state" in the refugee camps and neighbourhoods of West Beirut, as well as to the civil war which broke out in 1975.

But what makes Beirut so bizarre, says former New York Times bureau chief Thomas Friedman in his book *From Beirut to Jerusalem*, is the combination of getting caught in a cross-fire or in the middle of a bomb explosion, to the "ever-present prospect of dying a random, senseless death" and the instinct to "bring order and comfort to one's life amid chaos." Beirut's "flavour" is captured in the story of a socialite living along the green line who happened to be having a Christmas banquet when a prolonged exchange of gunfire and artillery barrage inconveniently broke out.

After waiting to no avail, she finally asked her guests: "Would you like to eat now or wait for the cease-fire?"

One of my favourite Beirut stories is Friedman's tale involving the gourmet Goodies Supermarket, which flew delicacies in daily from Paris. Goodies supplied Beirut's rich with caviar and smoked salmon. According to the legend, when a gunman tried to rob the cashier at Goodies, "three different women drew pistols out of their Gucci handbags, pumped a flurry of bullets into the thief, and then continued pushing their shopping carts down the bountiful aisles." Whether or not the story is true, it does give some sense of the atmosphere of Beirut and its mix of a weak central government, loads of money, high fashion and luxury, but also lots of drugs and weapons.

When the Israelis laid siege to Beirut, the people inside were both accustomed to random, sporadic everyday violence, and determined to live their lives as if nothing unusual was happening. Once back in 1983, I was astounded when one of my classmates was going back to Beirut for the Christmas holidays. Since the airport was closed due to heavy fighting, he was taking the boat from Cyprus. I asked him, "Aren't you afraid of all the fighting?" "No, not really, the biggest problem is the traffic jams across the green line."

SURVIVAL GAMES

The psychological games people played to cope with life in Beirut ranged from playing the "odds," which meant essentially trying to figure out what the odds are of getting caught in a cross-fire or in the middle of a bomb explosion, to the "conspiracy" game which meant finding or inventing explanations for the deaths of acquaintances and loved ones. A study by Richard Day, then at the American University of Beirut, found that those who survived the Israeli siege of Beirut the best were those who blocked out what they could not control and focused only on

those things they could control. This means that you decide what parts of your environment you see and what parts you block out. It goes something like this: "Here comes an Israeli F-15. Is it coming to get me? No. Can I do anything about it? No, then I will go out and play my tennis game."

Selim Nassib of the French daily Liberation in his book, *Beirut. Frontline Story!* describes "Madame Miza's" survival game. After months of bombings at any time of the day or night, she couldn't be bothered to get out of bed and go down to the cellar (kind of like having to get up in the middle of the night to go to the bathroom). Instead she would lie there and count the number of seconds between the flash and the explosion in order to determine how far away the bombing was, like we would count the seconds

By David Serlin

Cut-Out Identities

Cosmetic Surgery and Cultural Imperialism

In August 1993, Jonathan Preston Haynes, a self-confessed neo-Nazi and white supremacist, was tried and convicted for killing Dr. Martin Sullivan, a prominent plastic surgeon in Wilmette, Illinois, a wealthy suburb of Chicago. At his trial, Haynes explained that he resented Sullivan and all plastic surgeons because they transformed unworthy members of inferior races into people who resembled perfect specimens of the master race: "I condemn bleached-blond hair, tinted blue eyes, and fake facial features brought by plastic surgery… You fought World War Two against Aryan beauty. Stop feeding off Aryan beauty like a herd of locusts in a wheat field."

Haynes's tirade against cosmetic surgery is interesting, to say the least, for the ways that it uses World War Two as an historical marker. Probably unbeknownst to Haynes, it was during World War Two that plastic surgery techniques were refined, and perfected, so much that civilians could take advantage of them. Despite Haynes's white supremacist rhetoric, he is not alone in using race as a factor in the critique of cosmetic surgery. When, for example, in 1991, actress Kim Basinger took "bee-sting" collagen implants in her lips to make her mouth more full, an African-American writer for Ebony declared, "They took our music… now they're taking our lips!" Similarly, the strange case of Michael Jackson's successive surgeries have launched the careers of not a few journalists and cultural critics looking to expose Jackson as a traitor to racial authenticity.

One could argue about the racial and cultural politics inherent in stories like these, where what is at stake is not merely "fake Aryan beauty" but proscriptive ideals of appearance, normalization, beauty, color, shape and gender that seems, to me, not only Western but in certain ways particularly American. But to regard the results of cosmetic surgeries – such as nose jobs, eyelid surgery, breast augmentation or reduction – as a form of cultural imperialism in and of itself is only one part of the story, and only one way of explicating that story's power.

In this article, I will examine facets of the case history of the Hiroshima Maidens, the group of 25 Japanese women, burned and disfigured by the atomic bomb, who came to the United States in May 1955 for plastic and reconstructive surgery on their faces, hands, and bodies. As I will explain, by historically locating the Maidens as the subjects and objects of American medical science, I hope to demonstrate that the surgery performed on the Maidens has as much to do with ideas of beauty, appearance, and femininity as it has to do with the politics of science, foreign policy issues, and cultural imperialism at the height of the Cold War.

In 1949, Norman Cousins, editor of the Saturday Review of Literature, took a much-publicized tour of Japan, where his goal was to increase funding to orphanages and those made homeless by World War Two. Cousins's philanthropic work made him a well-publicized presence in postwar Japan, where his interests and concerns on behalf of war victims and children stood in stark contrast to the American military occupation of Japan, which lasted until 1952. In 1953, Cousins was approached by Reverend Kiyoshi Tanimoto, a Methodist-trained minister who offered community outreach programs to war victims from his church. One of Tanimoto's most special projects was a weekly support group he organized at his church for young women so badly burned and disfigured by exposure to the bomb that they were hidden from public view, often forced to live in their families' basements.

Tanimoto thought that, with Cousins's political sway, he could raise enough money for the young women to undergo plastic and reconstructive surgery that would enable them to live somewhat normal lives. The nature of the women's disfigurement was particular to radiation exposure: Skin was either burned off, or was irradiated to form keloid scars, or incredibly hard pieces of skin that often cemented arm or leg joints at right angles, and which made movement impossible.

In one case, a woman whose right eyelid had disintegrated in the heat and light of the atomic blast was incapable of closing her eye, which produced a steady stream of tears, a physical condition that served as a potent metaphor for the political condition of postwar Japan under reconstruction.

In addition to physical scarring, the women – all of whom came from poor families – had been relegated to dark basements and backrooms of houses, and were neither sent out to work for the family nor were they thought to be viable as prospective marriage material.

Moved by the plight of the young women – whom he had dubbed the "Hiroshima Maidens" – Cousins decided that the best possible medical care for the Maidens was in the United States. It might be worth saying that the term "Maidens" was normalized as part of the project's mission to rescue and transform these female victims of war. The fact that young Japanese women – and not young Japanese men or, for that matter, young Japanese soldiers – were brought to the United States made sense during what Sheila Johnson has called the "feminization" of postwar Japan by American popular culture. The American fascination in the early 1950s with Japanese architecture, flower arranging, Kabuki theater, and philosophy (in the form of books about Zen Buddhism by writers like Alan Watts, Jack Kerouac, and Allen Ginsberg), naturalized the Maidens' appearance, all of which were designed to replace the crafty, militaristic, kamikaze images of Japan with "soft" images in order to "repress wartime memories."

In 1953, Cousins contacted Dr. William Hitzig, his own personal physician at Mount Sinai Hospital in New York City, and asked him to assemble a team of plastic surgeons who would perform the necessary major and minor operations. Cousins's effort to relocate the Maidens to the United States for their reconstructive surgery is significant. I would argue that the celebrity status that the Maidens gained as a result of their surgery was based, at least in part, on the discourse of innovations and improvements that overwhelmed popular representations of medical science during the late 1940s and early 1950s. In 1946, readers of Life were told that, while "[in] peacetime there is no massive scale of injuries which approach the severity of battle… refinements in plastic surgery and the new methods of bone grafting and nerve repair will restore many victims of the violences of peacetime." This is partly because plastic surgery was promoted as an "art" developed as a medical specialty under the duress of wartime, and which bore the distinct heritage of military efficiency and expertise. The four primary physicians for the project – Arthur Barsky, William Hitzig, Samuel Kahn, and Bernard Simon – had all served in World War Two. In addition, Barksy, Kahn, and Simon were all board-certified plastic surgeons who resented their association with mere cosmetic surgeons, those "whores of the medical industry" who performed face lifts, breast augmentations, and the like.

Surgical feats, regularly linked to wartime advances and refinement in technology and technique, soon began to fill the postwar imagination as much as the promise of new superhighways or gleaming new appliances, and prompted Collier's magazine to pose the question: "Can humans be rebuilt?" The discourse of "expertise" espoused by American surgeons insulted the Japanese press, which accused Cousins and Tanimoto of luring the Maidens away for medical experimentation. Indeed, in 1952 a group of Soviet doctors approached the Maidens and told them they would perform their reconstructive surgery for free on the condition that they speak out against American imperialism and nuclear weapons testing. But long before Tanimoto or Cousins had even met the young women, Japanese surgeons who

survival of the FATTEST

the audience have all along been against Pupkin. When Pupkin pesters Langford's secretary not once or twice, but again and again, we are on her side and we suffer along with her. When Pupkin later gate-crashes Langford's country estate, the audience is again not on Pupkin's, but on Langford's side. As the plot unfolds, Pupkin reveals a bad case of social dyslexia. He is obnoxious, ridiculous, tactless, and pathetic. His attempts to swoon the girl he loves, Rita, are ungraceful, nerdy, and conceited. The people in the movie want nothing to do with him and the movie's audience cannot help sympathizing with them. Rupert is not likeable. He does not "deserve" and has not "earned" success. (Rupert's meticulously groomed hair and moustache, and his neat but slightly surreal wardrobe, establish a visual metaphor for his social dyslexia.)

But the story does not end when Rupert Pupkin is sent to jail. Only seconds remain of the film's running time, and yet a complete reversal of the plot—the peripiteia—is yet to come. In less than a minute we, the audience, are told the following: Pupkin spends his time in jail writing his memoirs. Because Pupkin's ten minute monologue was seen by an estimated 87 million American households, and because Pupkin made headlines and magazine covers everywhere when the media learned of the spectacular celebrity kidnapping, Pupkin already is a household name, and his book becomes a best seller. He is released from prison after less than 3 years, with hundreds of dedicated fans greeting him at the prison gates. In the last image of the movie, Pupkin greets the ecstatic studio audience of his very own nationwide television comedy show. Everyone who used to put him down now sucks up to him, simply because his notoriety and fame has made him bankable. This sudden and unexpected turn of events prove that the biggest joke of *The King of Comedy* all along was never on Pupkin but on us, the audience.

If you can't get what you want by going by the book, *you have to bend the rules*. Given the right circumstances, crime does pay very well indeed. *The King Of Comedy* is, however, not at all a film about decadence or moral decay in modern American society. The maxim "crime does not pay" is not challenged per se. After all, Rupert Pupkin is sent to jail. The film does, however, suggest the option of considering crime nihilistically as investment and commodity: Rupert Pupkin purchases the benefits in breaking the law, and invests for the future by doing time (just like Nelson Mandela—morals, motives, and goals aside). Once the price is paid and the debt to society is settled, Pupkin is free to conquer the very society he has trespassed against, going on to become an American hero and superstar. In many countries (those with no capital punishment or life-long imprisonment), someone like Pupkin could even use murder as a nihilist vehicle through which to achieve, in time, greatness and success.

This message is indeed subversive, but it would have been lost on the audience, had not 99 % of the film's running time been invested in establishing and insisting on Rupert's impossible character. It would have been just another American Dream success story, in which the talented and good-hearted hero—"undeservingly" held back by society and envious colleagues—refuses to give up, works even harder, and in the end, "deservingly," gets what he wants. Rupert Pupkin "deserves" nothing. As a comic he is mediocre. He is not funnier than any other wannabe comic, and he certainly does not possess the character and good nature of a person who the public "feels" has "deserved" success. Pupkin's personality ensures that neither idle chance nor luck, nor hard work and diligence, will win him any favors or privilege—not in America, nor anywhere else. The normal path to a career in comedy—via stand-up comedy clubs, television, and film—is thus never an option open to Rupert. Charitable or philanthropic organizations could not assist him in his repeated attempts to escape his social and professional predicament. Not even a brilliant piece on him by a Pulitzer-prize winning reporter could help him. Nor could, discouragingly enough, the institutions of democracy. No one will ever come to the rescue of a schmuck. In the minds of the public, there is no greater crime than to be, like Rupert Pupkin, a loser. The American Dream is not for the Rupert Pupkins of the world.

Historically, neglected and disrespected groups in society have, through legislation or revolution, worked themselves into political arenas, making society more responsive to their needs. For the Rupert Pupkins of the world joining such a group is never an option. Nobody wants them to join. To transcend the society and, not least, the personality of which he is a prisoner, Rupert Pupkin has to fight alone.

Fighting all your battles alone is hard, of course, but at least you do not have to submit to a group manifesto or simplistic common denominator compromises. He who conquers alone does not have to settle for membership in a society already defined and upheld by others. He can create a brave, all new world for himself, just as Jesus, Napoleon and Stalin did. Who would have thought: Rupert Pupkin—the Nietzschean, nihilist transgressor of democracy: Rupert Pupkin—der Übermensch.

FATTEST

Left: Cover from the Swedish tabloid Aftonbladet's Sunday supplement. Middle and right: Fake magazine covers featured in *The King of Comedy*

Fact: Martin Melin

September 1997. The Swedish media are going berserk. Details about a new television game show—yet to be aired—have been leaked to the media, and so enraged and appalled journalists that a nation-wide campaign to ban the show is started by the sensationalist evening tabloids. The show that has created such commotion, Expedition Robinson (as in Robinson Crusoe), is based on a format by a British production company, Planet 24 (original title of the format: Survive), in which sixteen contestants—adults of both sexes, of different ages, and from different walks of life—have been selected by a casting committee to spend six weeks during the summer of 1997 on an uninhabited island in the South China Sea. Everyone helps and shares in finding food and building shelters. A passive TV-crew is registering every step and every conversation, much like *The Real World*, MTV's popular show from a few years back. The object of the game and the program is to select one contestant as a modern-day Robinson Crusoe. He or she wins a substantial cash prize. In each weekly one-hour episode the television audience is invited to watch not only how the participants deal with their daily trials to find food (which turns out to be the contestants' biggest problem), but also to deal with damp clothes that never dry, shelters that fall apart, and of course the social frictions that emerge. There are also typical game show competitions, intentionally silly and tongue-in-cheek, including tropical island-style games such as bowling with coconuts. But the dramatic high point of each episode is the vote to send one contestant home. Each contestant explains why he or she thinks so-and-so should be sent home. The majority rules. Like ten little indians, they grow fewer with each passing program.

In the months between the pre-recording of the show and the actual broadcasting, something unexpected happens. The first contestant to be voted out and sent home, a young man, unfortunately commits suicide. The man's family blames the Darwinian process of selective survival, the vote to punish (rather than to reward) a member of the collective. Columnists and opinion makers join forces with the family of the deceased to stop the show.

In spite of everything, the first episode of Expedition Robinson is aired as planned on September 13, 1997. To lessen the attention around the young man who took his life, and in an attempt to muffle the expected outcry in the media, the provocative element of each contestant spelling out his or her reasons for wanting to get rid of a certain contestant is not shown. To no avail. The reviews are, as expected, devastating. The broadcasting schedule for the remaining episodes is halted and the television executive responsible is left with no choice but to "resign." Still, six weeks on location in the South China Sea costs money. Not to broadcast all episodes would be a waste. Presumably, each contestant has made a mature and conscious choice between the advantages (money, exhibitionism) and disadvantages (humiliation) of participation. This mitigates against the media's original accusations of Darwinian exploitation. After things have cooled off, the remaining episodes are finally aired, beginning October 4, 1997. At first there is some grunting in the media about this, but over time the aggressiveness dies down as the ratings for the series go up. As public opinion swings in favor of the show, the same sensationalist tabloids that cried wolf the loudest start doing phone-ins, interviews and biographical portraits on the contestants.

The reason for the show's popularity is the intriguing sociological perspective. In the first episodes, those voted out are not those who are the least successful at fishing or hunting or building huts, but those who are least liked, the misfits. Over time, voting patterns change, and the Swedish television audience is stupefied when the majority—the mediocre players—start to conspire against the strongest and best liked players. For example, the young man whom everyone expects to win because of his good nature, method, temperament and strength, is cast out at an early stage of the game. Scheming and intricate survival tactics lead to unexpected results: the fewer the contestants, the less predictable each vote gets. Fabulous entertainment.

December 13, 1997: The last episode of Expedition Robinson is broadcast. Martin Melin, a thirty-something chubby police officer from Stockholm wins the game and SEK 250,000 ($ 30,000). He has lost some 40 pounds (20 kilos) in six weeks. He is no longer fat. On the contrary, he flaunts an impressive torso. He is not anorectic-looking like the rest, he looks just right. Investing six weeks in starvation and total loss of privacy on a game show whose format has challenged every public notion of decency, good taste and political correctness, turned out to be an excellent choice for flabby Martin Melin. He is not only the champion, but he has completely reinvented himself. No longer the bloated lard-

Permanent Food

Based: Somewhere
Editors: Paola Manfrin and Maurizio Cattelan

Permanent Food *is a non-profit magazine with a selection of pages taken from magazines all over the world. It has been conceived and created by Dominique Gonzalez-Foerster and Maurizio Cattelan and is simply a collection of striking images. In a Debordian sense,* Permanent Food *is a second-generation magazine with a free copyright.*

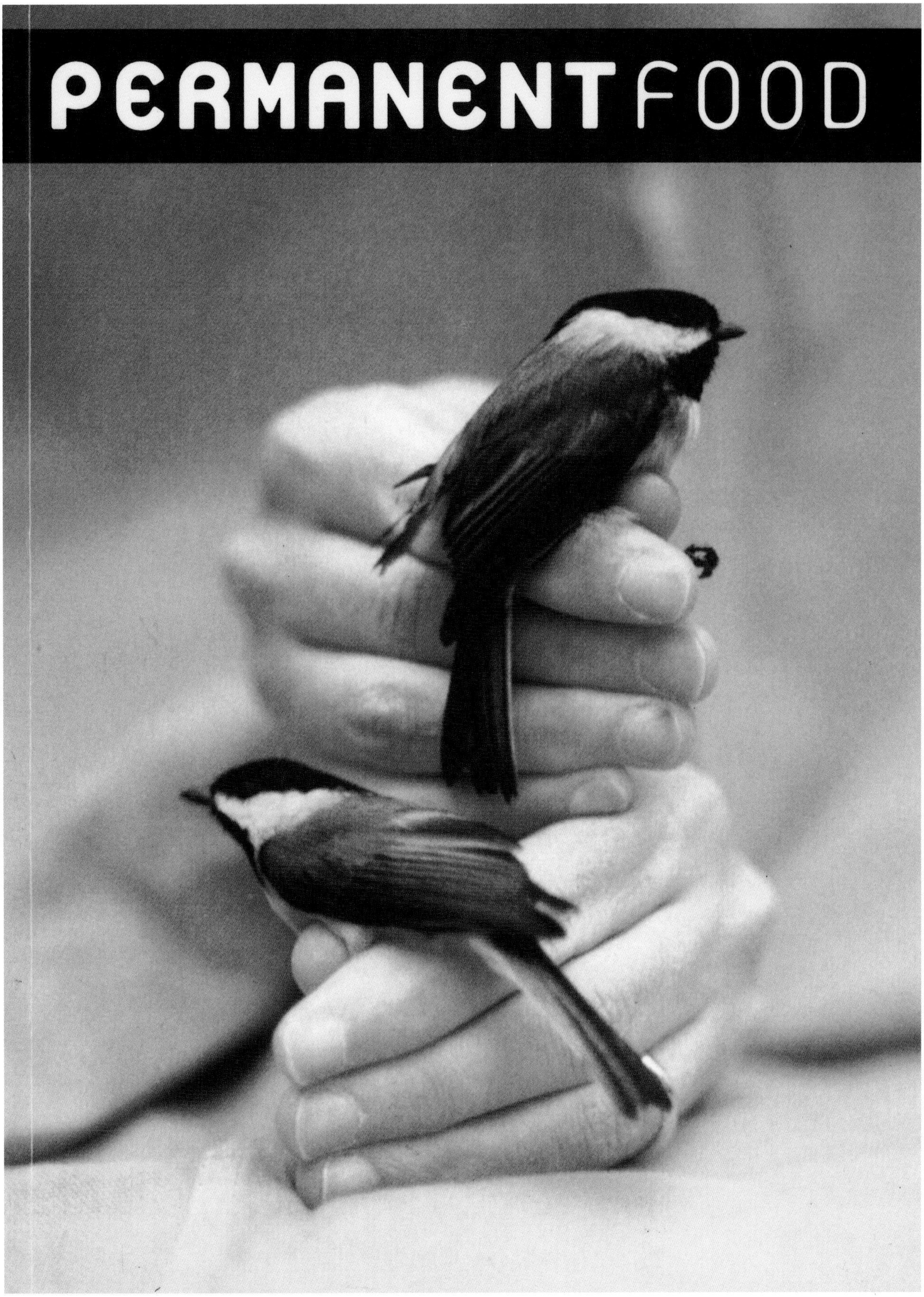
PERMANENTFOOD

Petit Glam

Based: Tokyo
Publisher and Editor-in-Chief: Co Ito
Art Director: Takaya Goto
Associate Editor: Kaori Tanabe

The history of Petit Grand Publishing, Inc. founded by us—Co Ito and Chinatsu Doi—in 1996 began with a tiny fashion magazine of postcard size. The magazine was originally named Petit Glamour, *(which means 'small' yet 'glamorous') and despite its fanzine-like production quality, it immediately became a huge hit, and all copies were sold out. After the successful first issue, in thinking about our future development, the new editorial concept was proposed: The key theme was 'kawaii,' (which literally means 'cute' in English). As the term accommodates such various meanings as 'beautiful,' 'small' and 'marvellous' etc. in Japanese, and thus is referred to as uniquely Japanese feeling, by compiling fresh and diverse ideas into a compact format, we sought to create a special package of different artistic expressions that would enhance and heighten the aesthetics of 'cuteness.' Aside from this proposal, the name of the magazine was changed to* Petit Glam, *and a new format (B6 horizontal size) was introduced as the standard format, and finally, each issue was designed to render a different packaging supplemented by the artist book project. Furthermore, Takaya Goto, a graphic designer living in New York City was invited as our art director. It was through these transformations, we had succeeded to create the visual magazine of exceptionally high quality.*

Rather than following new fashions or trends, our main goal is to create a 'new context' and 'new thinking style' and ultimately to propose 'new vision,' whether the topics we deal with are new or old. Indeed, this is how we could present our originality.

Meanwhile, our project also includes the publications of a film magazine entitled, Weird Movies A Go! Go! *with a special topic on films from all over the world, books of recently released films, photography books, and art books. It also extends to film distributions, which will start with Russian puppet animation,* Chebrashka *in the year 2001. All in all,* Petit Glam *will regularly include the coverage of all these future projects of Petit Grand Publishing, Inc.*

PetitGlam style culture fashion

no. 4

The Secrets of Chappie
Ikuo Ono Complete Works
Hiroshi Nomura Interview
Cris Moor
Buffaro'66
Playmobil

The Separate Volume
Strange Kinoko Dance Company + COUPDÉTAT
Shingo Wakagi + Yoko Omori
Motoko + groovisions + Hitomi
Kenshu Shintsubo + Umiko Yamada

Petit Glam Artist Book Series
Copy 3 by Leah Singer

VISUALOVELY ISSUE

Purple

Based: Paris
Publisher: Elein Fleiss
Editors-in-Chief: Elein Fleiss and Olivier Zahm
Art Director: Makoto Ohrui
Associate Editors: Laetitia Benat, Dike Blair, Jeff Rian and Bennett Simpson

In 1992 Purple Prose *magazine was founded by Elein Fleiss, its publisher, and her co-editor-in-chief, Olivier Zahm. They were supported by a group of like-minded friends, mostly from the art world. Initially it was a way to participate in the art world and to bring the art world into it. Eventually it expanded and* Purple Prose *spawned two additional magazines,* Purple Fiction *and* Purple Fashion. *The three magazines eventually turned back into one, book-sized, 450+ page edition simply called* Purple, *which brings together an even larger group of like-minded artists, writers, photographers, filmmakers, architects and musicians. Since the beginning the magazine's co-founders have curated art exhibitions in Paris, Geneva, New York, Copenhagen, Vienna, etc., including* L'hiver de l'amour *("The Winter of Love"), which opened at Paris's Musée d'Art Moderne de la Ville de Paris and traveled to P.S.1 in New York. In the year 2000, Fleiss and Zahm opened the remodeled Georges Pompidou Centre with a multidimensional international art exhibition* Elysian Fields. *Like the magazine, the exhibitions began with art and gradually brought in works and ideas from related peripheries, such as music, fashion and design. As* Purple *grew an office was needed. A space was found that included a storefront, which inspired the Purple Café. A combination café and boutique, Purple Café offers beverages (non-alcoholic), CDs, clothes, magazines, accessories, and pictures (unsigned) by photographers who participate in making* Purple. *A significant element of the magazine is its "look," which also evolved in concert with its content, which includes all the arts, design, street as well as runway fashion and themes in what is now the Prose section. Eighty percent of* Purple's *texts are in English, but its readers are international.*

Thus, the "look" grew increasingly photography-oriented in order to accommodate the inhabitants of a world freighted and immersed in pictures. Four times a year Purple *publishes a nexus of ideas and images that cross many borders and might very well constitute a language based on a "look."*

purple

Number 8 / Summer 2001
50 F

9 782912 684268

I'm ambivalent about why the world needs another designer. I see my clothes as somehow political.
I ask questions about morality, status, justice, ambivalence — often on an intuitive level.
I know that democratic fashion is a paradox. Fashion has more in common with fascism and
dictatorships than with equality and justice. I'm an idealist but not a perfectionist in my work.
Nor do I think that fashion is for everyone. Fashion is just another set of rules, which aren't so obvious
to anyone outside the fashion business. I'm very aware of the contradictions, since my designs are hard
to relate to if you're not interested in fashion. I get my inspiration from the ordinary and boring rather
than the interesting and beautiful. Things that are so common you don't even realize they are there.
So I go back to normality, where there is some air left and room to move. But what I do has nothing
to do with poor white trash or irony. I'm just fed up with all the design around me. You can't even go to
the bathroom without having to endure someone's designer toilet paper. I work with accessible,
everyday fabrics, and not precious designer materials. I also use something I call "aspirational" fabrics,
which lie about their true identity, and promise more than what they offer. I don't present customers
with a clothing solution. I am quite far from any solution. I ask questions about what fashion is.
I want to continue working this way, slowly but surely, with as little interference or pressure as possible.

Ann-Sofie Back

10 / Jeff / *The editor of your favorite magazine calls you and wants to meet you at a café at seven. What do you wear? What will you order?*
a) Nothing.
b) Everything.

11 / Lee / *Do drugs and sex go together?*
Yeah, but only with rock and roll. Ask Ian Dury.

12 / Jeff / *Would you have a relationship with someone you were physically attracted to but whose taste in food, drugs and/or clothes was uncomfortably opposite to your own? Which ones are most important? Rate them in terms of acceptability and tell us, if you can, why.*
This is a tough one. On the one hand, opposites attract. Or so the cliché goes. On the other hand, where would you meet somebody with an opposite taste? Not in your favorite restaurant, club, venue or bar, that's for sure. Even in a more public place it's pretty impossible to meet. Take, for example, a supermarket. While you are packing your trolley with veggie burgers, she'd be out there checking out carcasses. So maybe this mythical Person With An Opposite Taste is destined to never cross your path. Like some kind of dark evil twin or something.

13 / Bernard / *At what level do clothes determine desire?*
Below the belt.

14 / Bennett / *Do you take "seconds" when they're offered?*
Sure I take seconds. I even take thirds and fourths. But I don't like fifths.

15 / Claude / *Who do you sleep with after you take off your latest Hermès outfit, your new Miu-Miu shoes, your silky Gucci underwear and your timeless Chopard watch?*
Somebody who wears that kind of stuff only wants to sleep with himself, I'm afraid.

16 / Bennett / *Has buying things (food, clothes, even drugs) on the Internet/Web changed (or will it change) the way you think of shopping?*
Downloading food, clothes or drugs is still a problem for me. Maybe I need a quicker Mac.

17 / Elein / *Describe the restaurant of the future.*
An underground McDonalds on the nuclear ruins of a post-apocalyptic society.

18 / Kyle / *If the rock-paper-scissors game was changed to food-drugs-clothes, what would beat what? Why?*
I'm still trying to figure out who would beat who if the game was changed into Freud-Marx-Sartre. After that I'll come back to your question.

I wish more people, in general, would do magazines as a pastime, like gardening.
by <u>Amy Fusselman</u>

Amy Fusselman is a writer living in New York City.

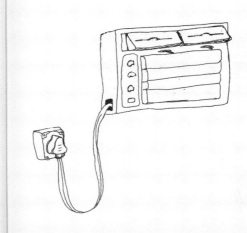

Questions d'éléphant
Siam l'éléphant interroge Jean-Luc Vilmouth

Siam : En quoi ton travail parle-t-il aux éléphants ? Jean-Luc Vilmouth : Dans l'histoire du pot*, c'est un éléphant qui est à l'origine de l'empreinte qui va devenir un récipient. Nous avons des histoires en commun, réelles ou imaginaires comme le Livre de la Jungle mais qui en disent long sur la convivialité, les interactions et la communication possible entre les humains et vous. J'essaye de révéler cela. Je pense que l'on ne prend pas assez au sérieux tout ce que vous pouvez nous apprendre. Comment prendre une douche avec sa trompe par exemple ! Ou plus sérieusement vos capacités de guérisseur. Actuellement de plus en plus de chercheurs, neuropsychiatres, pédiatres se passionnent pour vos capacités thérapeutiques.
Crois-tu à l'utilité d'une nouvelle Arche de Noé ? Et quelle serait alors sa forme ? Est-ce que tu as entendu parler de Biosphère 2 qui est un peu une continuation de l'idée d'Arche de Noé ? Construire un monde artificiel sans danger en excluant certaines espèces est un peu une illusion. Une Arche de Noé conçue par l'homme n'est parfaite que pour lui. Cependant si je devais imaginer une nouvelle Arche, je prendrais pour point de départ notre monde avec une conscience globale, un équilibre, un partage et une meilleure répartition, pour que tous les êtres vivants sur cette planète aient leur place.
Penses-tu qu'un jour les éléphants pourront marcher sur la lune ? Je préfère te voir dans ton milieu naturel.
Dis-moi, le fusil est-il une augmentation de l'homme ? Malheureusement pour toi, oui.
Lorsque nous nous rencontrons, as-tu le sentiment de parler avec le dernier éléphant ? Et toi as-tu le sentiment de parler avec le dernier homme ? Je pense que nous faisons tous les deux partie d'espèces menacées à plus ou moins long terme.

Me prends-tu pour une carte d'identité de la vie, une masse de fiction, un réservoir d'histoire ou une trace du monde ? Tout cela en même temps et à ce sujet, j'aimerais citer une histoire chinoise. C'est l'histoire d'un roi qui demande à quatre aveugles d'observer un éléphant. Le premier touche les jambes, le second l'oreille, le troisième la trompe et le quatrième la queue. Après cette expérience, chacun raconte à quoi ressemble un éléphant. Celui qui a touché les jambes dit : "un éléphant, c'est quatre colonnes". Celui qui a touché la trompe : "un éléphant, c'est un câble". Celui qui a touché l'oreille : "c'est un grand éventail". Celui qui a touché la queue : "c'est un large balai". D'ailleurs, c'est drôle de savoir qu'en chinois, éléphant et imagination sont un seul et même mot.
Crois-tu qu'un jour tu pourras entrer dans la peau d'un éléphant ? Je crois que je peux me rapprocher de toi jusqu'à un certain point, nous ne pouvons entrer dans la peau d'un éléphant, comme tu dis, qu'en fonction de nos connaissances et de notre intuition. Alors entrer dans la peau d'un éléphant ne peut être pour moi qu'une fiction, mais une très belle fiction. Pourtant il y a interaction entre l'homme et l'éléphant et nous avons des connexions et une histoire commune qui remontent très loin. Quelquefois je me demande pourquoi nous nous efforçons de chercher des traces de vie sur d'autres planètes, alors que la diversité du vivant sur terre est tellement passionnante. Pour protéger la diversité de ce monde, les animaux et les hommes devraient dialoguer plus souvent ensemble comme nous le faisons aujourd'hui.

Interprète : Stéphane Camille

* Découvrir II. Comme dans l'histoire du premier pot (1987), où une femme, après avoir dégagé une empreinte d'éléphant dans la boue pour porter son eau au village, avait laissé ce récipient près du feu et découvert le lendemain un pot solide.

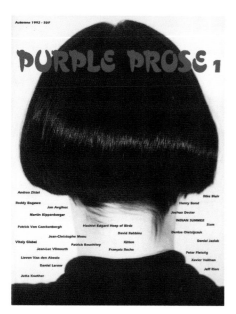

Andrea Zittel
Roddy Bogawa   Dike Blair
          Jan Avgikos   Henry Bond
Martin Kippenberger   Joshua Decter
                              INDIAN SUMMER
Patrick Van Caeckenbergh   Siam
          Hachivi Edgard Heap of Birds
Jean-Christophe Menu   David Robbins
                              Denise Oletsijcauk
Vitaly Glabel   Daniel Jaslak
          Patrick Bouchitey   Kitten
Jean-Luc Vilmouth
          François Roche
Lieven Van den Abeele   Peter Fleiszig
          Daniel Lerner   Xavier Veilhan
                              Jeff Rian
Jutta Koether

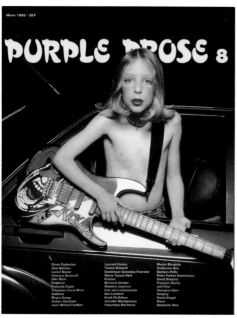

Blues Explosion   Laurent Fuzlon   Martin Margiela
Alan Belcher   Toland Grinnell   Guillaume Nez
Lionel Bovier   Dominique Gonzalez-Foerster   Barbara Polla
Vanessa Beecroft   Gloria Toyun Park   Peter Parker Experience
Dike Blair   Kramer   David Robbins
Dogbrel   Bernard Joisten   François Roche
Francois Cadel   Stephen Jsannon   Jeff Rian
Timonaze Gurui Mora   Ines van Lumsswerde   Georgina Starr
Gudvine   Alix Lambert   Surgery
Moyra Davey   Scott McGehee   David Siegel
Anders Edstrom   Jennifer Montgomery   Weon
Jean-Michel Fradkin   Yazumasa Morimura   Benjamin Weil

MARTIN MARGIELA / A group of enlarged generic garments, which includes men's clothes,
such as trench coat, jacket, vest, shirt, T-shirt, sweater, as well as women's second-hand dresses and slips.
All the garments in this group have had their form and original size transformed by hand and enlarged to size 74.
(Belgian designer based in Paris)

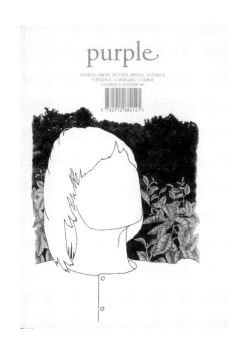

Re-

Based: Amsterdam

Editor-in-chief/Designer: Jop van Bennekom

Executive Editor: Julia van Mourik

Editors: Lernert Engelberts, Arnoud Holleman

Photography: covers, Anuschka Blommers/Niels Schumm

Publisher: Artimo

Frequency: 3 times a year

www.re-magazine.com

mail@re-magazine.com

Is this a magazine?

From its very beginning Re-Magazine *has not been bound to a certain lifestyle group, neither has it been linked to any specific professional field. Instead* Re-Magazine *is about life in general. RE- started in 1997 as 'Daily Life Magazine', not intended to be a vehicle for the extreme, the new, or the stereotypical, but for the marginal, the ordinary, and the common. In the summer of 2000 Re-Magazine was re-introduced with* Re-Magazine #4 'The Boring Issue'. *Followed by #5 'Re-connect Yourself.', #6 'The Information Trashcan', and #7 'Re-View' which was released in Autumn 2001.* Re-Magazine *is a fast-growing independent magazine, with a vast international network of contributors—fellow communication explorers in a variety of disciplines from photography and fashion to ICT.* Re-Magazine *is neither a lifestyle, fashion, art nor a design magazine. In fact it's a magazine in-between all other magazines.* Re-Magazine *is about escaping the status quo, as existing formats and genres no longer suffice. It is looking for a new 'code', a language in-between disciplines, a new common ground. Therefore,* Re-Magazine *needs to re-invent itself every time; a magazine as an adventure. Re- communicates the necessity from which it is created: A magazine that doesn't make any compromises, a vehicle for ideas and concepts, a tool to investigate what we're interested in. With every issue* Re-Magazine *explores, investigates and researches a contemporary theme. The making of the magazine is part of the research project, which leads to editorial experimentation and new editorial forms.*

Re-Magazine #6
From Amsterdam NL
Spring 2001
The Manic Issue
Hfl. 17,50 / 8 Euro

Not.

RE—

©

THE
INFORMATION
TRASHCAN

Page 1 continues on page 2.

Having no idea what to do. Taking the car at night,
trying to get away from it all.
Shooting pictures in the dark of things you can't see.
Searching for moments in time without a story, devoid of memory.
Meanwhile having doubts about the whole concept.
Photography: Tim Gutt (The Valley) and Jop van Bennekom

This is climax.

do.

Having
no idea what
to do...

*Taking the car at night & taking
pictures in the dark of things you can't
see. Trying to get away from it all.
Searching for moments in time
without a story, devoid of memory.
meanwhile having doubts about
the whole concept.*

Picture One

Attempt

**Hello,
this is an infotorial.**

**Please,
add message here.**

Bread

Levi's® RED™

Meanwhile... stress at the office of Re-Magazine
in Amsterdam. Jop (wearing a Levi's® RED™ 1st
comfort W32 L32 male model jeans) is searching
for something extremely important, something
very crucial. In mid-search he suddenly forgets
what he's looking for

Attempt

13 Attempts.

98

Ref.

Based: Tokyo
Publisher: Yutaro Oka
Editor: Keiko Maeda
Art Direction: Synchro Design Tokyo
www.bea.hi-ho.ne.jp/synchro/

Ref. *is a music lovers' fashion magazine which publishes the fashions of the audiences who go to live concerts. Picking up on the excitement of rock and fashion tribes of audiences,* Ref. *highlights the exaltation of live concerts from a position that draws a line between other famous magazines. By using many young photographers and with a policy of enjoying the actual moment,* Ref. *has become a spirited visual magazine.*

Ref. *stands for reflection. It also refers to the meaning of reflection such as influence, reverberation, image, etc..*

The fashions of the music lovers are influenced by the music, but they also have an effect on the music itself. There are many kinds of music like punk, techno, reggae, etc. They each have an original fashion tribe and the power to influence the fashion scene. Also, new fashions are expected to break out from the new music discovered by a new generation of listeners.

This magazine only focuses on fashion that comes out at 'live concerts'—a key concept of our magazine. Fashions on the street and fashions seen in night clubs are close, but we separate them from fashions of live concerts. This said, this magazine will not include CD rating and feedback or interviews.

Recently Ref. *has gathered data and photography from both major and minor live concerts without discrimination. And we have added a serial pages theme from our project 'sending from audience.'*

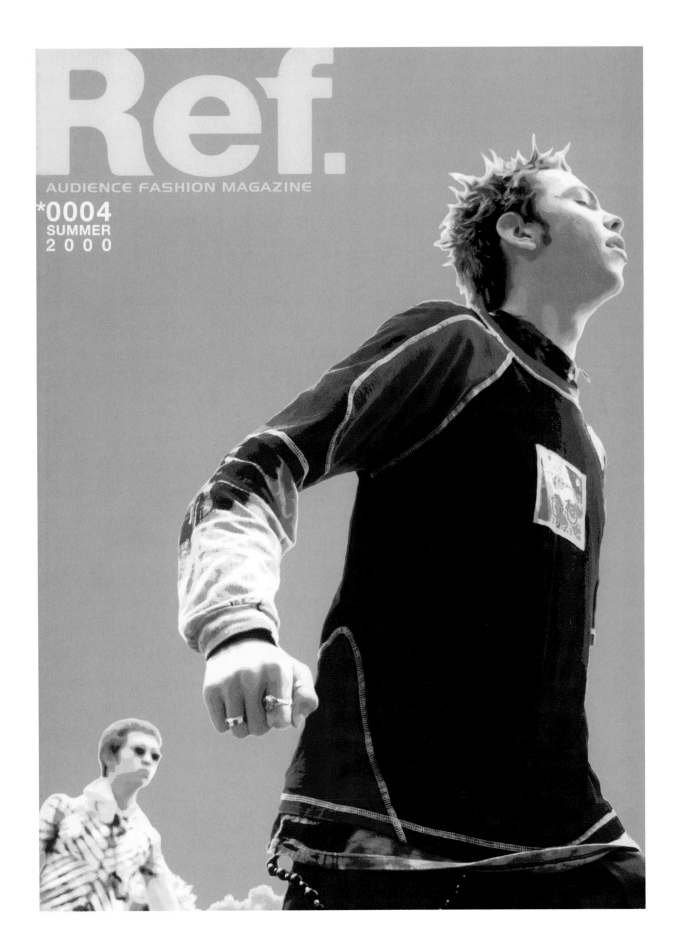

Ref.

AUDIENCE FASHION MAGAZINE

*0004
SUMMER
2000

JUMPING audience of

GEORGE CLINTON & P-FUNK ALL STARS

at YOKOHAMA BAY HALL / 12 Feb 2000 photography by KEN

L06R07

アルヒノオト
その❶グレイトフルデッド
Illustration & text by Koji AZISAKA

Sec.

Based: Amsterdam
Editorial Staff: Yolanda Huntelaar, Roosje Klap, Martien Mulder, NFI, Richard Niessen,
Martine Stig, Viviane Sassen
Design: Yolanda Huntelaar, Roosje Klap, Richard Niessen
E-mail: sec@ok-ams.nl

Sec. was started by a group of photographers in 1997, from the idea of creating a space for autonomous work by various artists. It should be considered as a collection of unpublished personal images that were created without any commercial purpose. Sec. has always been created without any advertisements and with no concessions towards the concept.

Sec. is made, distributed and designed without any interest in money by a varying group of photographers (Martien Mulder, Martine Stig, Viviane Sassen) and graphic designers (Roosje Klap, Odilo Girod and Esther de Vries); all from Amsterdam, Holland.

Sec. is doing very well. We have had several publications in a.o. Adformation Magazine, IM, Blvd., Parool. *It was also nominated for the Design Prize Rotterdam. We have had exhibitions in Amsterdam (the Consortium - 1999, the Stedelijk Museum - 1999), Rotterdam (National Photo Institute - 2000-2001) and in Antwerp (Fish and Chips - 1999, Visions - 2000). This fall, we will represent the Netherlands at the Herten International Photo Manifestation in Germany. Our publications have always had a very portfolio-like character, but for our last three publications, we have been trying to work from a certain theme, trying to enlarge our vision on society and art, and maybe even make a statement, although we still are keeping our free 'stage' for various international artists.*

Jan Rothuizen

Karen Heuter

Persin Broersen
Reymond Schobert

Johannes Schwartz

Sannah de Zwart

Art direction:
Arlette Muscher

One photo was interpreted in text by
four different authors. Each of these
texts lead to images by 3 different artists
(for translations: www.veenman-druk/sec).
This resulted in Sec.6

Sec.6

Bert Houbrechts

Martine Stig

Arjen Mulder

Mascha Smitt •

Devon Ress

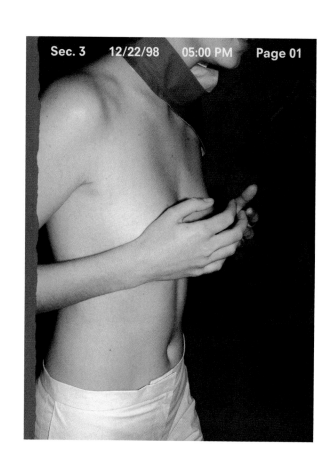

Sec. 3   12/22/98   05:00 PM   Page 01

Sec. 4   28/05/99   05:00 PM   Page

Martin Parr
Mona de Valère

Naoyama Serranaino

Gialo Giscol

Orino Pratt

Philip van dem Boesche
with Sara de Bondt
& Spahni Nys

Sebastien Biaselage
& Nasako Wolf

Taende-tri

Vivvine Sassem

Paul Brasasat

Sec. 4   28/05/99   05:00 PM   Page 01

c. 4   28/05/99   05:00 PM   Page 15

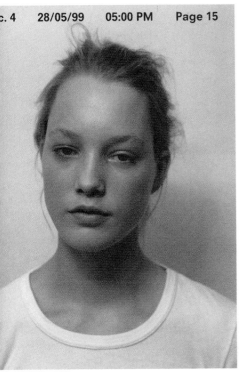

Very

Based: New York
Editor: Uscha Pohl
Photo Editor: Angela Hill
Art Director: Uscha Pohl
E-mail: very@upandco.com
www.veryUP.com

VERY *is a magazine based on the concept of a curated group exhibition in a gallery. Artists working in different media and creative fields, are featured quarterly within the boundaries of 44 substantial matte pages.*

The VERY *design offers simply the bare essentials in the attempt to enhance the original artwork while leaving it mainly untouched.* VERY *subtly ignores the customary rules of periodicals and instead sets the tone of an open global creative mix.*

Distributed internationally since 1997, VERY *was created by Uscha Pohl and photographer Angela Hill.* VERY *is published out of* UP & CO, *New York: a Tribeca gallery / art space showcasing solo and group shows, with its own* UP & CO *men's and women's fashion line designed by Ellis Kreuger and Uscha Pohl.*

VERYstyleguide, *is your indispensable, pocket size, bi-annual "Where Fashion meets Art" guidebook for New York and London. Our special every issue is the global section—where key players in the know take you to special places.*

VERY*styleguide.com takes off from there by providing links to a whole online fashion and art network. And this is just the beginning... Discover, enjoy, find what you need!*

VERY

$6 £3.5 13DM 35FF

0 74470 93663 3

Display until 15 August 1998

Opposite page:
Black Shirt   Veronique Leroy
White Linen Trousers   Veronique Leroy
Golden Necklace   Marie-Hélène de Taillac

This page:
White Long Sleeve T Shirt   APC
Black Trousers   Vintage Comme des Garçons

Following pages:
Silk Handprinted Top   Aurora dei Carraresi
Silk Handprinted Wrapskirt   Aurora dei Carraresi

THE GO BETWEEN

VERY **16**

PHOTOGRAPHY ANGELA HILL

ART DIRECTION

ANGELA HILL & USCHA POHL

City School

Photography   Angela Hill
Styling   Sara Humberstone

(opposite)   Trousers   Comme des Garçons
                      Comme des Garçons
(this page)   Coat   Joseph

VERY

US $6

VERYstyleguide

111

Visionaire

Based: New York
Editors and Co-Founders: Stephan Gan, James Kaliardos, Cecilia Dean
www.visionaireworld.com

Visionaire *is a multi-format album of fashion and art produced in exclusive limited editions. Each issue is hand-numbered and released as a collector's item. Since its inception in the Spring of 1991,* Visionaire *has offered a forum for works by both famous and emerging artists from around the world as well as personalities, fashion designers, art directors, and image-makers: Richard Avedon, Steven Meisel, Mario Testino, Bruce Weber, Cindy Sherman, Nan Goldin, Mary Ellen Mark, Madonna, Catherine Deneuve, Fabien Baron, Helmut Newton, Jean-Paul Goude, Bill Cunningham, Ellen Von Unweth, Alexander McQueen, Mario Sorrenti, David Sims, Andres Serrano, Peter Lindbergh, John Galliano, Pierre Le-Tan, Jean Phillippe Delhomme, Mats Gustafson, Balthus, Martin Margiela, Roni Horn, Tony Oursler, Pipilotti Rist, Philip-Lorca diCorcia, Ross Bleckner, Karl Lagerfeld, Philip Taaffe, Craig McDean, Raymond Meier, Francois Berthoud, Helmut Lang, Barbara Kruger, Hiomix, Stephane Sednaoui, Nick Knight, Ruben Toledo, Wolfgang Tillmans, Gregory Crewdson, Frank Gehry, David LaChapelle, Andreas Gursky, Steve Hiett, Alex Katz, Inez Van Lamsweerde & Vinoodh Matadin, Toyo Ito, to name a few.*

Published 3-4 times a year, Visionaire *features a different theme and format each season. Artists work in collaboration with* Visionaire *to produce their personal interpretations on a theme, and are given unparalleled freedom to push* Visionaire*'s different formats.*

Close to You
Jeff Rian

It's almost 20 years since Karen Carpenter purged herself for the last time. February 4, 1983. Curled up on the floor in her parents' house, all skin and bones, dead of a heart attack induced by two years of anorexia nervosa, a martyr of fame and desire.

The Carpenters' album *Close to You*, (1970) had the song "We've Only Just Begun" on it. Written by Roger Nichols and Paul Williams for a "soft sell" bank commercial, it became the first in a string of 16 Top 20 hits and the sale of about 100 million records worldwide. They were the best-selling group of the 1970s. Karen was the drummer. But in the band's first review she was described as "the cute but chubby" Karen. The description stuck to her. It chased her to her grave. There were more albums in her, more songs to sing, more tours, more management decisions. But the songs, her image—they weren't working anymore. In March of 1983 she would have reached the christological age, a third of a century: an age to die and to be remembered—an age still young enough to be put back together in collective memory, like Humpty Dumpty, like A.E. Housman's "To An Athlete Dying Young"—little chubby Karen, the anorexia poster mummy, days shy of 33.

Karen withered during a major lifestyle swing. Lots of things were changing. Postmodern design and architecture updated art deco, the first really modernist era, born in Paris in the mid-1920s. In 1983 the stock market was a year into an unprecedented rise. The Sony Walkman, nouvelle cuisine, jogging gear, seltzer and designer clothes were captivating imaginations. The magazine *Self* came out about that time. A few lines of cocaine made the night sparkle. Therein were the seeds for Martha Stewart's project-oriented, yuppie-preppie entertainment management, shown in magazines and on TV. A feeling of economic renewal was in the air, whose dark side—a plague in the making—was the identification of the AIDS virus in 1981. By 1985, however, the first Graphical User Interfaces (GUIs) would come on the market. Gooeys, as they were called, were computer mice, with mouse pads (their own little turning ground). Everything since Gutenberg was about to transform.

This was also about the time when the models in fashion magazines started spreading their legs to give a racier edge to a picture and shop mannequins were given nipples. I'd wondered who or what propelled those views and where it was going. Was it a combination of lifestyle, cocaine and aerobics? Was it the Scarsdale diet? I remember asking the lingerie editor of *American Vogue*, a friend, what she thought about all that. She said she hadn't noticed. I also remember asking an editor of the art journal *October*, around 1982, what he thought about painting. He said it was dead. I imagined him following the logic of his magazine, for which painting was in fact dead. But this wasn't much long after David Salle and Julian Schnabel and all those Italian and German painters exploded onto the scene. So, in other magazines, certainly in the art market, painting was very much alive. As for the models, they started looking like mannequins stripped bare.

Magazines flourished, too. They reprocessed the present and the past through computer technology. Books were repackaged to have pictorial designs. Lifestyle itself became a new industry for the service economy. It seemed like shopping would save the world from another economic slump. Karen wasn't yet a memory (as she was to me, inexplicably, the morning I was invited to write this text).

Poor Karen had probably had enough trouble dealing with her image, how she looked, how much she weighed, her calorie intake, her future, her youth. The "look" she chased was born in a review: a rear-view image that reverberated in a feedback loop in her imagination—an image that she measured against herself and other magazine creatures. As the reverberation increased she lost touch with her self and maybe got trapped in a viscous schizomogenic circle. The feedback loop accelerated. Thinness has to be maintained. To be thin is to be thinner. Already she was hooked on devotion. She'd risen high enough to lose a sense of humor about it. She was aloft in the aeries of image and success. She saw herself in magazines.

Anorexia nervosa purportedly affects about one percent of adolescent females in the United States, about 10 percent of whom die of self-starvation. Reasons are unclear. Karen Carpenter was just another product of an adolescent lifestyle that is projected on all adults to be forever young, forever thin. She happened to be trapped by it. Adolescents in the late 19th century, by contrast, were obsessed with being adults. Young men grew beards and dressed like their elders. Women sucked it in to be buxomy and steatopgic-looking. But in an age driven by pop art's tenets (Richard Hamilton's list included youth, gimmicks, sex, speed, big business, and fast consumption), dressing down, jogging and staying young—and thin—gave the magazine industry themes, issues and contexts. They gave burgeoning adults like Karen an image to aspire to. Anorexia was just one late 20th century theme, perhaps one that corresponded to the romanticism of tuberculosis in the previous century. Saint Theresa's ecstatic romance with Christ and Simone Weil's visionary duty toward mankind come to mind. Weil's life also ended in self-starvation. It's too cynical to call them martyrs. Yet their deaths contributed to our awakening. The information each generated in religious fervor, in the genius of their beliefs, in the depths of their sorrows, in the vastness of their hearts and the fullness of their souls, filled imaginations with empathy. In that regard Kurt Cobain's self-immolation bore the same reliquary wonder for magazine readers today, offering an image to contemplate—as if Edvard Munch's angst-ridden "screamer" were a scraggly genius suicide, luridly delineated in articles and in the news.

Those who stretch their self-limits stretch our imaginations. The information involves real-life scenarios drawn out in detail, with real potential set against a reader's imagination. Such charisma fuels a magazine's internal engine. Magazines bellow those flames. Not only are ecstasy and self-immolation news, they reek of emotion, belief, abandonment, the psychology of the self. They offer shards of identity to grasp at and cling to like a karmic logo.

****

Magazines—like shopping catalogues and guidebooks—are named and designed with completeness in mind. Their purpose is to flesh out the contours of little calculated worlds that are sold back to consumers. Magazines are generally dictatorial, not democratic: one vision propels them, one editorial policy informs them, one idea keeps them identifiable. They are made to attract a particular audience, befitting a moment in time, a *Zeitgeist*, a social stage, a population group. They are categorized by market genres and a librarian's logic. What they show and discuss is tailored through the editing, cropping and highlighting of points of view to fit a focus. All of them have their biases and angles of perspective. By and large they convey real information about the real world—even if the information is fictive or skewed. Editors and journalists are supposedly objective. They try to be even, fair, balanced, orderly. But even the most balanced article cannot complete a picture. The whole truth is all but impossible to flesh out. Distortions are inevitable. Yet we rely on behind-the-scenes editing. We trust that magazines are what they are supposed to be: authoritative, informative, entertaining, funny, specific—and that they will present themselves as accessories, as friendly little snacks that feed us with information about the lives of artists, criminals, saints, sinners, celebrities and underdogs. We pay for them, endorse them, increase them, adorn and honor them. Like clothes, we enter them, put them on, wear them a bit and then throw them out.

Their attraction draws upon ingredients found in classical art and the canons of beauty. All except one: magazines can be balanced, elegant, well ordered and well made, but they lack proportion, depth, dimension. They are allure exaggerated. The perfect girl next door. The perfect lover. This attraction is further complicated by advertisements, which always exaggerate the good points and downplay the bad. Advertisers, of course, support magazines. Selling ads keeps magazines alive. So the characteristics a magazine draws upon, from and back to their particular niche, are inevitably distorted.

Magazines live and die with their constituencies, the social milieus and the public consciousness that brought them to life. *Rolling Stone* and *Mother Jones* were products of the sixties counterculture. Magazines like *I-d*, *Purple* (where I am an editor), and *Barfout*, among others, began in the '90s as fanzines. They evolved from the counter culture of home computers. Often new magazines are bought up by larger publishing houses. Magazines are bought, sold, made over and killed, sometimes to resurface for another aesthetic life, another moment in time. A lot of seemingly successful magazines, such as the *New Yorker*, lose money but are maintained for their prestige by publishers (Condé Nast) that flood the market with a variety of magazines to spread out the risk and the profit potential. Fanzines survive either because they have benefactors, some family money, or their creators have a day gig and work a lot of late hours.

But something happened between 1982 and 1992, which changed more radically between 1992 and the present. Not only did computers revolutionize the publishing industry, QuarkXpress and Pagemaker programs paved the way for the fanzines and self-made designers of the early '90s. By then page layout was being done by home-based freelancers, called formatters. For the big publishing houses, formatters needed to understand editors' specs, or specifications in order to turn copyedited manuscripts into printable files. Specs were written in very specific language, as complicated as legalese, with the type and layout measured in picas and points. Picas are one-sixth of an inch, based on 12 points, and typewriters that print ten characters to the inch. A code phrase like "10/12.5 fl-left Garamond" told the formatter to use 10-point Garamond type on 12.5 point leading, measured from the imaginary baselines of the letters, one line above another, with the text set flush left. That language is also changing. GUIs changed the game. Amateurs changed the rules. Specs haven't been the same since. Terms like "cutting and pasting" are done with mice, not scissors and glue. Designers and editors had to learn to use computers or get another job. It didn't matter how talented they were.

No publisher before 1990 would have allowed a formatter like David Carson, designer of *Raygun*, to annihilate line-spacing with such radical intensity. Magazines not only changed their style with computers but also reflected shifting reading patterns. Punctuation loosened up to fit patterns more common in speech. More and more, em dashes (a dash like this "—," the length of a capital M) started appearing. Style sheets were rethought so readers could scan without stumbling on speed bumps like too many commas or, god forbid, those academic semicolons.

The fanzines were also unencumbered by editors, proofreaders, fact-checkers, advertisers' pressure and censorship. They were like friendly letter bombs, full of attitude and style, not unlike the broadsides of Samuel Pepys's age: half political, half censorious, half barb—and maybe half conscious of what was being said. They were made by individuals, not market analysts. They created their own niche. The fanzines became a feeding ground for the major magazines. Yet their effect had a longer reach and what appears to have been a real effect on the glossies. One mutated into the other. Fanzines grew. Bigger magazines changed their style.

Yet everything has its lifespan. Economists talk about the law of diminishing returns: supply and demand increase until products start to lose cost-effectiveness. So while postmodernism flourished between the rise of the Dow-Jones stock index in 1982 and the stockmarket crash of 1987, during the economic lull between 1987 and 1992—a time when home computers became cheaper and more available—the stage was set for a change in style and an unprecedented proliferation of magazines. As the economy rebounded, beginning around 1992, magazines began to appear in profusion. This profusion, or at least its current style, also seems to be peaking—if it hasn't already.

When fanzines like *Purple*, *Self-Service*, *Barfout*, etc., started to hit newsstands, they brought with them a new generation of photographers, such as Wolfgang Tillmans, Jack Pierson, Mark Borthwick, Cris Moor, Anders Edström and Hiromix, among others. Their style, in turn, showed models in simpler poses, often frankly naked instead of sculpturally nude, sometimes with a musician's brazen attitude, and often in an everyday setting instead of a photographer's backdrop. Styles changed. Many of those visual styles were linked to attitudes and styles in the new music, independent rock, techno and hip-hop, as well as independent film. These styles—along with the writing, stories, angles, attitudes and even a sense of taste—looked outside current fashion and mainstream trends. (A couple years ago I wrote about these changes in an article called "Paranoia Soft".[1]) Gradually, a change in style was inspired by a fanzine attitude that favored a visual style over an editorial policy.

In the past half-decade, many magazines have followed this primarily visual trend, now to the point of saturation. New magazines started to look alike; one stole from another. There were differences (I have my own prejudices), but by and large the trend was stylistically similar even when the content differed. Following an earlier decade of lifestyle invention, a decade of new magazines now leaves us in a bulimic state. There are just too many. But surely a new trend is now gestating, waiting to be noticed.

Purge and gorge. Purge and gorge. Fill us up, put us on, wear us, take us away.

The dramas enacted—the purges, fits, gaffes, crimes, misdemeanors, kindnesses, immolations, catastrophes and turn-ons—incite desire, fear, caution, passion, anxiety, even indifference. Magazines extrude all the valences of a stylistic swing. They tally vices and virtues, losses and gains, beatitudes and curses. Advice and dissent mingle with all that we are, own and aspire to. Magazines do it all. They thrive on volume and easily starve.

****

Let's be crass and imagine an ideal life as something like Calvin Klein's: the beauty, the jeans and bare feet, the cover of *Vanity Fair*, the bottled water and chopsticks, the pristine loft, the country house, the teeth, an ascetic life with a red Ferrari. Sometimes I think a lot of magazines would like the world to live a combination of Swedish and Japanese lifestyles: fish, nature, shopping and style. They'd like shoppers to have better taste and to be better bred. Everyone would have a G4 laptop and shop at organic greengrocers. Wouldn't that be grand?

Zen Buddhists and 12-step programs often preach a yin-yang concept of acceptance and letting go. Accept things as they are because you cannot change them. Live in the present. Accept who you are and who you are not. Identify your feelings. Take the bad in with the good but don't cling to either. Let go of feelings that are disruptive. Sleep when tired. Eat when hungry. Don't get carried away with expectations. Don't let one picture (or one review) decide your fate. This is sound advice for staying out of the sauce, off the needle, away from the credit cards and out of a narcissistic vortex. Karmic acceptance can help you to let go of obsessions, bad habits, nervous ticks, anxieties. Staying grounded is the key, paying for it a requisite. Maturity is a goal.

But it's the extremes that tell us who we are and where not to go. The Saint Theresas, Simones, Karens and Kurts extended themselves in thoughts and emotions, in acts and reactions. They died prematurely. (Before they matured?) What led them to ecstasy and passion? Was it love, pain, abandonment? Or reckless, feckless commitment? Had denial become a river, to invert a bad joke?

Magazines shower us with lives as lived and with life as it might be. They show who and what some are while telling others who and what they are not. This in fact is a virtue. But only if the examples don't go too far overboard, which they almost always do, endlessly repeated, one version out doing the other. Fortunately, there are a lot of choices. For all their fancy images and social distortions (intended and not)—and for all their non sequiturs, jump-cuts, disjunctions and truths—they contain the seeds of human potential. Flipping through magazine pages is not only a lesson in life but also an analogue to the way we think in hieroglyphic jump-cuts and disjunctions. In the mishmash of stories, ads and pictures, truth, falsehood and potential are sought and sometimes found. Magazine editors try to fit images and words to patterns they sense in the world at large. Some get it right.

Flipping through a magazine involves a kind of escape from and toward something or someplace else. Something new, different, interesting is potentially available. There is an elegance in this kind of patterning. This kind of breezy scanning is not the in-breathing gaze of an aesthete before a work of hieratic art—the balance, order and proportion of, say, *The Winged Victory of Samothrace* (a work I never quite got). Nor is it the sublime beauty of, say, a dark brooding storm full of theater and dazzle in a painting by Caspar David Friedrich (which I always found a bit kitschy). But a real storm is, in fact, looming, threatening and intense, as is a magazine photograph of such a storm. Magazines have the potential to inspire and to terrify with startling beauty or with wickedly bad news. They excite us to diddle and wank ourselves to orgasm. They are little, calculated havens of brief ecstatic escape. Ecstasy involves escaping and succumbing. Magazines offer constantly changing patterns and styles that move along in a wavelike, particle-filled consistency. They change constantly. They are ever-renewed. Riffling the pages of a favorite magazine is an escape quickie. Saint Theresa might have transported herself by dandling the familiar rosary in her pocket. Simone Weil might have risen up in her feverish diaries about "the needs of the soul." Karen and Kurt were immolated by split images of themselves. We find them all in the pages of magazines. Ecstasy, transformation and death.

In Isaiah Berlin's book-length essay *The Hedgehog and the Fox*, he borrowed an idea from a Greek poet named Archilochus, who said, "The fox knows many things, but the hedgehog knows one big thing." In North America, a hedgehog is a porcupine, whose one defense is a hide full of needles. Berlin's idea was that some of us search for one unifying principle while others look for many ends and means, which, unfortunately, often lead to contradictory conclusions. He suggested that Tolstoy did both, using voluminous descriptive details to compose an epic picture of history. Tolstoy wanted to know why things happened. But you can't always know why. Historians have yet to piece together the real causes of the Great War of 1914–1918. (That was a case where a really epic war actually seemed to "break out.") Tolstoy didn't see the Whole Truth, either. He saw what Berlin called "the many"—a collection of images and ideas that create a larger picture or pattern. To Tolstoy, knowledge was empirical: the more we know about something, the more evidence we have to show, the more inevitable things will seem to be—which, if you think about it is more idealistic than he might have admitted. Tolstoy's one big idea needed myriad little details to elucidate it. He wrote great big books to make something clear. His heroes have glimpses of "what happened," maybe a picture of something true, but only glimpses, not entire histories. And the one Big Idea escaped both Tolstoy and his heroes—even though the books conveyed them. But that's art's way of being clear, not history's.

As is generally the case with unified theories, no sooner have you pinned down something here than a complication crops up there. Physicists have learned that energy is transferred in both waves and particles. They have seen one and the other but not both at the same time. Historians try to be thorough, carefully examining a period, footnoting sources, reading everything they can find. Journalists try to be factual, concise. Yet total coverage is difficult at best, even though larger patterns are sensed, artistically.

Magazines probe the very reaches of our symbolic perceptions. They examine every activity the world has to offer. Newsstands are both museums and theme parks. Their shelves offer a grab-bag version of the grand unified theory. Each section is an environment, a niche, a specialized population unto itself.

Magazines are as prolific as an insidious virus or a great invention. They are stylized and style-oriented and copied endlessly, making them powerfully redundant. Redundancy—the repetition of words and images—is a primary ingredient in communication. Repetition creates patterns. Pattern recognition feeds on redundancy. Like all mass media, magazines base their messages on a shallow familiarity with a person, place, thing or event. They involve distribution networks that start small and, out of economic necessity, feel they must grow to thrive. The more familiar something is, the easier it is to ingest. This is where knowledge becomes complicated.

Repetition doesn't create depth or greater understanding. It creates familiarity, with only the potential to understand more deeply. On one level, repeated images of persons, places, things, events or styles become patterns. The patterns are constantly renewed, updated and restyled. That doesn't necessarily bring them beyond a first order of familiarity. Hearing about something and seeing it again and again says something about the pattern but not necessarily about the thing itself. The pattern becomes redundant but the story has yet to be fleshed out. Stories are often too complicated to understand without consulting more than one history book. Even then, clarity can be a kaleidoscope of opinions whose patterns have to be decoded. The repetition doesn't always lead to clarity. There never seems to be one unified theory— even about the Great War. Karen Carpenter seems to have been trapped in a feedback loop (a repeating pattern) over the word "chubby." She could neither accept it nor let it go.

James Joyce called a newspaper a "microchasm" of human life—a small but endless labyrinth of human interest stories. A newspaper's columns form its architecture. Its stories reflect a cross-section of planetary life, vivisected and isolated for perusal. Newspapers and magazines are basically the same in every language. You don't have to know Chinese to know where the news, sports, entertainment or classified sections of a Chinese newspaper are. They all have pictures and advertisements, and generally they speak about the same topics. Celebrities are often the same everywhere. Magazines are more specialized. But they pretty much look the same all over the world, even in Japan where they are read backward. And, of course, ads are still interspersed with the news and entertainment.

In the eons before books, newspapers and magazines, cultural lore was passed along the generations in mythical tales, with heavy archetypes playing various informative roles. The different characters were described by their social identity. Native Americans gave themselves animal names. Greek gods hurled thunder, had winged feet and so on. Their women were virgins, mothers, whores or clairvoyants. Men were hunters, bosses, warriors. Today, uniforms still label soldiers, priests, workers, business people, hippies, punks, and Mafiosi. When early cultures made an image of a person, they depicted the person ideally, not individually. They were unanimous societies and had no interest in privacy or difference—just as science is unanimous in its ultimate application for us today. From a traditional perspective, individualism was secondary to the society's well-being. To behave otherwise was to be insane. And rather than idealizing the future (as we might in science fiction), they idealized the past of their ancestors upon whose behavior, though mythic, they based their own.

In the entertainment age, the heavy archetype has returned. The celebrity is an exaggerated citizen, a person wearing sunglasses, a heliotrope reaching for the light, flying to heaven, sometimes going down in flames. Advertising has recuperated the winds of rhetoric and the tribal drum to attract attention. In the few are the many. In the media are the messages. "The medium is the message," to repeat McLuhan. The air is filled with logo waves and particle images. Planet Magazine. Planet TV. Planet Net. Celebrities are the heavy archetypes. Politicians are intermediary guardians kept in check by journalists. They are all mediums operating in the media we depend on but don't entirely trust. One way to approach magazines—all of them—is to be a fox, a hedgehog and a student of Zen: accept "the many" and the over-thralling abundance, and remain aware of patterns while remembering to look for informing details. Pick them up. Treat them as candy and watch out for the sugar. Keep a steady aesthetic distance. Accept them. Edit them as your own. Be Magazine. And Magazine. Forget Magazine. Nirvana Magazine. Nothingness Magazine.

Karen Carpenter fell into her own "microchasm" when the word-image "chubby" hit her square in the identity. Maybe if she had been born in the hip-hop generation she could have been a chubby drummer/singer and not been trapped in a feedback loop replaying thinness as a theme.

Themes change. Images change. Photographers change. Styles change. The Internet has been designed to come in closer than books, magazines and TV. Where will that take us? Away from each other? Out of our bodies, toward population implosion? Closer and closer till we merge and agglomerate and the celebrities are forgotten and we all become distracted abstractions, citizen particles, citizen waves, never one and the same but closer and further away?

Paris, May 2001

1. "Paranoia Soft" first appeared in *Flash Art* magazine, Vol. XXXII, No. 209, November-December 1999, pp. 89–91, then in a slightly different form in the catalogue, *Supersonic Transport*, 2000, for a show at the Charles H. Scott Gallery in Vancouver, B.C. Basically it was about style, photography and independent film in the early '90s.

Robin Mitchell

Vancouver Soundscape Project

The soundscape is any acoustic field of study. We may speak of a musical composition as a soundscape, or a radio program as a soundscape. We can isolate and study the acoustic environment as a field of study just as we can study the characteristics of a given landscape.
R. Murray Schafer "The Tuning of the World."

In the spring I recorded soundscapes around Vancouver, also taking photographs of each location. Later, examining what I had collected, I found similarities between our soundscapes, landscapes and weather.

Vancouver is a softly coloured city: green, blue and grey with flashes of yellow and red, more vibrant in relief to the constant cloud cover that diffuses the sunlight. This weather muffles our city's sounds—sometimes the sounds of the rain and traffic overwhelm all the others. We had an unexpectedly dry spring this year, making these soundscapes and landscapes clearer and brighter than they might have been otherwise.

The Vancouver Soundscape Project *is a small book divided into two main parts, and comes with a CD of sound recordings. The first part of the book contains a series of photographs. The second part contains a corresponding series of simple collages based on the recordings, as well as the shapes and colours in the photos. The appendix of the book includes an image of each location taken from a Vancouver city map, and a ballpoint pen diagram of the city's sonography from my notebook.*

The idea for the project came from two main sources. One was the World Soundscape Project, *based in Vancouver in the mid 1970s, which documented endangered soundscapes around the world. The other was the work of the situationists, in particular their concept of the derive, which Guy Debord described as "a technique of rapid passage through varied ambiences involving playful constructive behaviour."*

at right: #52 Bus, False Creek

Hussein Chalayan show s/s 2001.

GLAMOUR PART ONE:

PEOPLE

Outtakes from a film by TINA AXELSSON,
MARIA BEN SAAD and STEFANIA MALMSTEN.

JACKY

Jacky Mpiolani-Piolard, Rue Guy Môquet, Paris. July 14, 2000.

– I think that certainly glamour is
  important. Because it's so rare. I mean,
  like beauty or like intelligence or
  great, physical, athletic ability,
  glamour is attractive because it's like
  a black swan or something. It's very,
  very unusual and it's something that
  people respond to strongly. Although

00:01:32:14

STINA

Stina Johnson, Karlavägen, Stockholm. November 1, 2000.

they may be resentful and angry about
it as much as they are attracted.
                    VALERIE STEELE

– In my experience, because I don't really
know people with money, I would say that
glamour often occurs in people without
money, because they are perhaps forced

00:02:16:07

KAMEL

Kamel Dridi, Karlavägen, Stockholm. December 10, 2000.

to pretend a little bit more. To imagine
themselves in a different way than their
circumstances outline for them. I think
people with money are equally as capable
of producing glamour. But I tend to
associate it more with people who started
without such favourable conditions.

BERNADETTE VAN-HUY

Sophia Kokosalaki show s/s 2001. Masaki Matsushima show s/s 2001. Shelley Fox show s/s 2001.

- I am interested in people who want to be, but fail to be, glamourous.

                                ANN-SOFIE BACK

- I always remember as a kid, every once in a while my mother would go to a party and she would get dressed up and she would have her hair done. And she would put on

00:04:15:58

Yuko Yabiku, The Pineal Eye, London. September 25, 2000. Eva van Straelen, Kammenstraat, Antwerp. Mars 3, 2001. Paulina Stoltz, ICA, London. September 25, 2000.

a nice cocktail dress or sometimes even an evening dress – we're talking about the 1950s, 1960s when I was a little kid. I remember thinking ah, she was so beautiful. In reality, she was just my mother, she probably looked like hell actually, but the reality was that I perceived her as glamourous. And she

00:05:22:09

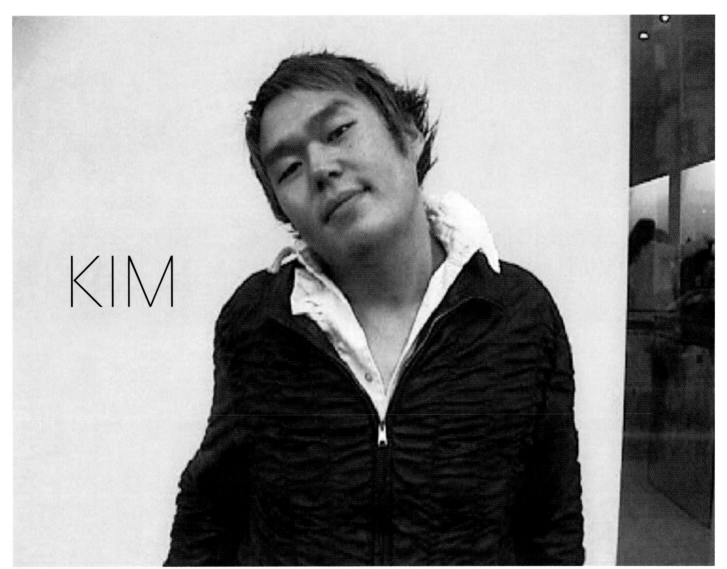

KIM

Kim Do Hyon, Rue Etienne Marcel, Paris. July 3, 2000.

perceived herself as being glamourous.
Because it took her out of where she was
everyday. Which was as a housewife.
RICHARD BUCKLEY

– It's a way to show yourself respect.
(C'est une façon de se mettre en valeur.)
LAMINE KOUYATÉ

00:06:42:19

CONNY

Conny Bloom, Highbury Islington, London. September 27, 2000.

– I don't believe that glamour exists
physically. Because as soon as you're
close enough to touch it, it ceases
to exist.

ANN-SOFIE BACK

– Clothes don't make a person glamourous.
It's the person that creates the

00:07:04:31

SARAH

Sarah Wauters, Kammenstraat, Antwerp. Mars 3, 2000.

glamour. People create the allure,
the mystery, the thing that you want,
the thing that draws you to them.
RICHARD BUCKLEY

– It's how you insist on a life that
isn't really your life.
BERNADETTE VAN-HUY

GLAMOUR PART ONE: PEOPLE was filmed in Antwerp, London,
Paris and Stockholm during 2000 and 2001. The quotes
on these pages are from interviews conducted over the
phone with Ann-Sofie Back, designer; Richard Buckley,
editor in chief at Vogue Hommes International; Lamine
Kouyaté, designer Xuly-Bët; Valerie Steele, museum
director at the Fashion Institute of Technology
in New York and Bernadette Van-Huy, editor in chief
at Made in USA Magazine.
GLAMOUR PART ONE: PEOPLE is produced by PIPEL© with
support from the Swedish Film Institute. Photography:
Tina Axelsson. Interviews: Maria Ben Saad. Graphics:
Stefania Malmsten. The full length version [8 minutes]
of the film is available at www.pipel.se.

00:08:16:11

WWW.PETIT.ORG

Petit Glam

CONCEPT & TEXT: **CO ITO** DESIGN: **TAKAYA GOTO**

HURRAH FOR HOMMA CAMERA'S MCSISTERS PHOTOGRAPHY: **TAKASHI HOMMA**
STYLIST: **SETSUKO TODOROKI** HAIR & MAKE UP: **HIROMI CHINONE** MODEL: **YUMI SHIMIZU** Yumi Shimizu at Kamakura photographed by Takashi
Homma, taken from "Petit Glam no. 6." This photograph is titled, "Hurrah for Homma Camera's mcSisters!" This photo session evolved into his photo book project, which is currently in progress.

NEW YORK BEAT
JEAN-MICHEL BASQUIAT IN DOWNTOWN81

Downtown 81 is the only film starring the artist, Jean-Michel Basquiat, who died at the age of 27. The film includes footage of such musicians and artists as Debbie Harry, Arto Lindsay, John Lurie and Kid Creole, as well as Andy Warhol visiting backstage, and a young Madonna. This visual book is a rare photographic documentation of the New York art and music scenes of the Eighties, with an essay written by Glenn O'Brien.

CINE CARNET 001
QUI ETES-VOUS MR. FREEDOM?
IRONICAL MOVIES IN 1960–1970

This premiere publication of the Postcard Magazine series commemorates the screening of *Mister Freedom*, directed by photographer William Klein. With a touch of pop-agitation, this extraordinary film parodies the social and political climate of the time symbolized by the outbreak of the Vietnam War. Scenes with various actors, including Philip Noiret and Serge Gainsbourg wearing costumes and fighting each other are a deluge of visual beauty.

PHOTO BOOK
THE VIRGIN SUICIDES

This photo book compiles various beautiful scenes from Sofia Coppola's directorial debut, *Virgin Suicides*. Active also as a photographer, Coppola selected these images by herself, a gem of unique visual beauty filled with the charm of young girls. One of Francis Ford Coppola's (Sofia's father) favorite books.

CINE CARNET 002
GASPER NOE'S WORLD
FROM CARNE TO SEUL CONTRE TOUS

This book, entitled *Gasper Noe's World*, is the second publication from the Postcard Magazine series. Gasper Noe made his debut as director with *Carne*, a bizarre film about the story of a mute daughter and her father who is a butcher. His new film *Seul Contre Tous*, a sequel to *Carne*, picks up where the earlier film left off. It is an unsettling love story with a shocking conclusion. Included are various archival materials, such as an interview with Noe, conducted by artist Takashi Murakami.

FILM BOOK
LA FILLE SUR LE PONT

This is a film book of *la fille sur le pont*, directed by Patrice Leconte, the master of the French Romance film, and starring popular actress, Vanessa Paradis. Features B&W film stills from this love story about Adele, a girl who wants to be loved and yet has no luck, and Gabor, a side-show knife thrower, as well as interviews with Leconte and Paradis.

CINE CARNET 003
GHOST WORLD
THE PORTRAIT OF TEENAGE GIRLS WHO LIVE USELESS

Terry Zwigoff, who filmed *Crumb*, a documentary about underground comic artist Robert Crumb, made this great teen film, starring actors including Thora Burch (*American Beauty*) and Steve Buscemi. Based upon the original graphic novel by Daniel Clowes, with unique cinematic details only made possible by Zwigoff, *Ghost World* is now available in book form.

STYLE TO KILL
BRANDED TO KILL – VISUAL DIRECTORY

Seijun Suzuki is a cult filmmaker, respected by filmmakers like Quentin Tarantino, John Woo, Jim Jarmusch, and Kar-wai Wong. This visual directory features a filmography of *Branded To Kill,* a classic film of Suzuki's aesthetics, accompanied by a DVD compiling ten original previews of his films.

VINCENT GALLO
1962-1999

This is the artist book of multi-talented Vincent Gallo, whose *Buffalo '66* became a huge hit in 1999. He directed the film, played the main character, wrote the screen play and did the soundtrack. Included in this book are photos from his childhood and his earlier period as racer, musician and artist, as well as those showing his friendship with Jean-Michel Basquiat, Winona Ryder, and Johnny Depp, accompanied by his own comments.

YASUZO MASUMURA RETROSPECTIVE

Known for his modernistic direction in such films as *Tsuma wa Kokuhakusuru, Quicksand* and *Tatoo,* Yasuzo Masumura is one of the Modern Japanese film makers who created a new type of Japanese cinema, overthrowing the melodramatic quality of traditional cinema and instead asserting the fusion of intelligence and emotion. Originally published as a catalogue for his Retrospective held in 2000, this book features a long interview with celebrated actress, Ayako Wakao. Wakao has starred in twenty of his films and her outstanding partnership with Masumura is remembered in the history of the Japanese Cinema.

PICTURE FRIENDS 002
IL GIRO DEL MONDO DEGLI
INNAMORATI DI PEYNET

It is really amazing that the only film of French painter Raymond Peynet was an animation made in Italy in 1974, and furthermore, it is truly delightful that this animation film is scheduled for re-screening in Japan. The picture book of this animation, a fantasy of lovers traveling beyond time and space in search of true love, is scheduled for publication in Fall, 2001.

REVENGE OF MODERNIST
KO NAKAHIRA RETROSPECTIVE

Ko Nakahira's Retrospective was the first of the retrospective screenings of Modern Japanese directors. Nakahira remains one of the most important film directors. His *Crazed Fruits* influenced the French *Nouvelle Vague.* In Japan, *Only On Mondays* starring the fairy-like actress Mariko Kaga, made a revival and prompted the reassessment of his works at his Retrospective held in 1999.

PICTURE FRIENDS 001
CHEBRASHKA

Chebrashka, made between 1969 and 1974, is a Russian puppet animation film (first distributed by Petit Glam Publications) directed by master animation filmmaker Roman Khachanov, mentor of Norshtein. It is truly a masterpiece of Russian animation films. The picture book of this film, available in hardback, is the first publication of the Picture Friends series.

TRANSPARENT PAGES ARTWORK: TAM OCHIAI

Tam Ochiai is a Japanese artist living in New York City, whose *White Book* was published as a supplement to Petit Glam no.3. Based on this book, Ochiai proposed to design transparent pages for this collaboration project with Petit Glam.

NAEF

Introduced for the first time in Petit Glam no. 3, Neaf was further featured in Petit Glam no.6. Our cover story was about a visit under the guidance of founder Mr. Kurt Neaf, to the Neaf factory in Switzerland, which produces high quality toys with a superb sense of design. This visit was also an opportunity to meet Neaf's designers, Mr. Peer Clahsen and Mr. Antonio Vitari. We are planning to publish a visual book to introduce European learning toys within this year.

LANCE WYMAN

Lance Wyman, a master artist in the world of sign design, was commissioned to design pictograms for the 1968 Mexico Olympics. The cute pictograms he designed for The National Zoological Park Washington include all the elements essential for visual communications. His story was featured in the "Paradise in Pictograms Issue" of Petit Glam no. 3.

PLAYMOBIL

Playmobil is a popular German learning toy, like LEGO. In Petit Glam no.4 various characters from Playmobil were combined to produce an original pictorial story. New models come out every year, but the older models have softer forms and look cuter and adorable. The model in the picture is a limited edition designed for Lufthansa Airlines, available for sale on the plane.

THE CONTRAST OF COLORS

Although Johannes Itten's *Art of Color* is considered the best text concerning color theory, *The Contrast of Colors* written by Elen Marks is a Science book that attempts to demonstrate color theory by using transparency films. Using this book as a sourcebook, Petit Glam no. 5 is entitled, "Individual Colors Issue," featuring various stories revolving around color.

RUBIK'S CUBE

Rubik's Cube was made by Erno Rubik, a lecturer at the Academy of Applied Arts and Crafts in Hungary, as an actual model to construct mathematical ideas in 3-D form. It became a huge hit around the world as the best puzzle of the twentieth century. Currently Petit Glam is checking out this amazing toy again, and is planning to feature it in the next issue. Incidentally, the photo shows a Cube made in France and a 'Magic Snake'.

BRUNO MUNARI

"Creativity that everyone would have as a child is really important," said artist/graphic designer Bruno Munari. The picture books and toys as well as educational materials he designed are full of remarkable ideas that stimulate your brain and hands, and thus are fresh surprises giving us a joy to learn. I PRELIBRI, once published by recently revived Danese is a sourcebook for Petit Grand Publishing.

STRANGE KINOKO DANCE COMPANY

Dance performance is Petit Glam's continuing interest, and it finally crystallized in "Pleasure Holiday of Strange Kinoko," a Petit Glam Extra that accompanied Petit Glam no. 4. This small photo book features the unique collaboration between a Strange Kinoko Dance Company, literally known for their strange and cute choreography and performance, and talented young photographer Shingo Wakagi.

MARIMEKKO

Marimekko, a long-established Finnish textile and clothing company, after passing through several trends, made a huge break again. Such talented designers as Maija Isola and Fujiwo Ishimoto, breathed new life into Marimekko's nostalgic textile design. There is a special 32-page coverage of Marimekko in Petit Glam no.6. *melooni* was also made into a poster.

UMIKO

A fourteen-year-old girl whom we met at the start of Petit Glam Publications, has grown up to be twenty years old. *Umiko* is a gorgeous photo book that tells a story of this young girl who was born near Lake Geneva in Switzerland, and now lives in Kyoto. What lies beyond her lingering gaze? All photo pages are super-gloss coated, adding an astonishing feeling of space.

CHAPPIE

Chappie is a character produced by groovisions who also participated in the exhibition, *Super Flat*. Petit Grand Publishing owns a mannequin of its earliest model. Petit Glam no.4 has a special feature article on Chappie. The baby doll costume in which she is dressed was actually worn by Christina Ricci for the test shooting of *Buffalo '66*.

KISHIN SHINOYAMA

Kishin Shinoyama is one of the internationally renowned Japanese photographers along with Nobuyoshi Araki. His artistic achievement is culminated in his so-called, 'Idol' portraits. These portraits of young girls, which Shinoyama started in the '70s, still remain fresh and glamorous. Its abridged version entitled, *Gekisha-Bunko* (The Pocket Book of 'Action' Photography) is his classic and an inspiration for Petit Glam Pictorial series.

TAKASHI MURAKAMI

Takashi Murakami is an artist who has also gained international recognition as producer/curator with his concept of 'Super Flat.' Convinced of a good partnership, Murakami introduced Petit Glam's Art Director, Takaya Goto, to the publisher, Co Ito. Without Murakami's insight, Petit Glam would not have been born!

MANON ARTWORK: WOO

For Petit Glam no.6 entitled, "Future Interior Issue," we selected as a main visual feature, Manon, a graphic pattern designed by WOO, a New York based interior designers collective. WOO simply sells their design concept and the buyers are given the liberty of using such concepts according to their own need. Using this pattern, Petit Glam produced packages, posters and cardboard boxes.

VERY

A PERSONAL QUEST

USCHA POHL

PRESENT, PAST AND FUTURE

When I started VERY (with my friend, photographer Angela Hill), no one asked me why. People were just generally skeptical.

Looking back, I cannot blame them (as of course I did then). You only dare things when either you know exactly what you are doing or nothing at all. In my case, it was the latter. I knew what it was like to be a fashion designer and didn't want to be one. I was much happier becoming an artist/ editor/publisher/gallerist/teacher/part-time designer after all, and all at the same time.

Within this mix, the magazine is essential and very close to me—it is a "state" governed by rules of my making, as well as an entity in its own right, removed and yet familiar, strangely resembling a "best friend" you turn to for advice and consolation, and to find new answers to the same questions.

Through the magazine I can find new perspectives on life and its issues and play with ideas. Combine beauty with thought, the frivolous with the essential, the real and the fictional. Create something rich that has not one but many meanings, a platform for ideas. Document incidents, experiences, creative expressions in a new hybridized culture that stems from a global world with all of its inherent contradictions.

As VERY was created, it didn't occur to me to model it on a predecessor. VERY was to be a personal quest, coming as close in form to a subjective journey as possible. By going straight to the writers and artists, in essence cutting out the "middle man," contributions became collaborative and direct.

Photo: Angela Hill. Cover VERY 8.

Photo: Brut DeCoffrage. Uscha Pohl holding VERY 5 at the launch party VERY at Marie-Hélène de Taillac Paris, 1999.

The big difference between VERY and other periodicals only became apparent to me when the first issue came off the press. When Angela and I snuck up to the WHSmith magazine display discreetly arranging VERY 1 on the shelves alongside the other mags…, well, it just looked VERY different.

As a stubborn teenager in the '80s I had spent lone weekends staring at the ceiling, furious that I was supposed to choose ONE path as a "career"—one job to learn rather than many. It was so limiting, so impossible to choose. Fifteen years later, technology had made it possible, I could physically, professionally, acceptably do more than one thing, renaissance seeming reborn.

New technology has made magazine publishing accessible to "everyone." Starting out as budding editor/publisher/art director as a graphics novice with no prior experience in the field, an understanding soul had to even spell the word "zip" for me. I purchased a computer. I set out to sell ads for something I had nothing to show for. Four months later, with some very helpful help from my friends, I was holding VERY 1 in my hand: September 5, 1997.

Today, choosing the magazine format for my quest I find myself in the great company of many. But what came before?

As I am writing this, the laptop goes "ping": a new email. It is from Sarah Shatz who's been working with me on our one-year-old "cash cow baby"—the supplementary publication, VERYstyleguide. I had told Sarah about an article. Curious, I had read:

"By the way, Interview magazine was co-founded in 1969 by Warhol and Gerard Malenga, who was a Factory fixture. Bob Colacello was the editor from 1970-1983…just watched a great documentary called *Andy Warhol: Superstar*, and Bob said that Andy was relentless, a real work-horse, and would call him at 5am demanding to know, 'Bob, have you gotten that Estée Lauder ad???' See? Never changes, Uscha…"

Some things never change—Which do?

Artist Stephen Willats started CONTROL (magazine) in 1964 from his studio in central London. CONTROL deals with the issue of how art manifests itself and looks at its social function. The specially commissioned contributions of the guest artists therefore deal with the present and project into the future.

700 copies are printed each time. Some back issues are still available: issues 4 ('68), 5 ('69), 6 (71), 14 ('91), 15 ('98). Issue 4 featured here I just bought at Printed Matter in New York, some 33 years after publication. Today, in July 2001, Stephen Willats is just about to get issue 16 back from the printers.

Calling Stephen for this VERY interview, I am surprised to find that many of the questions I am about to ask are actually also dealt with in the upcoming issue of CONTROL. So I am very intrigued now. I will have to get the new CONTROL. But here are Stephen's answers, first.

CONTROL

Magazine. 1964–present.
Edited and published by Stephen Willats, conceptual artist, based in London. CONTROL Magazine; By artists, with artists, read by artists, art theoreticians and maybe some others.

Uscha Pohl: "Control" as a title is provocative and has many associations. What did it mean for you, what was the main reason for this choice?

Stephen Willats: Initially, the word "control" just seemed to be very modern, reflect the times very well whilst being nicely controversial at the same time. "Control" as a word, has been traditionally understood as one entity determining another. In the early '60s the idea came about that one could exist as a self-organizing system that determines itself, its own parts. So art could move away from being "institutionalized." Separate from the museums and galleries and white walls, artists could determine the rules for themselves in the fabric of life–hence taking "control."

The word as a title is subversive, representing a self-empowering, a "mutiny" to the system, and in its polemic attracted a lot of attention, particularly in the '70s.

UP What spurred the idea of the creation of "Control?"

SW There was this feeling that visual art was finished. From being very specialist at the outset of the '60s, where there was no communications between disciplines such as mathematics, psychology, engineering and art at all, suddenly everything was meant to be one. The mid-'60s was an era of interdisciplinary ideas, the vanishing of boundaries between the domains of musicians, philosophers. Everyone thought of themselves "artists," and everything could be art. What constituted the difference?

There was no single answer. "Control" was created out of the void of a platform for artists to express themselves, outside the traditional form of galleries/museums.

UP Were there other magazines/periodicals/publications around at the time that you could reference?

SW The only "art periodicals" I recall around in London at the time, were "Craft" magazine (arts + crafts), "signals," a journalistic magazine, "Studio" on English pottery. Control was the first artist manifesto set to disseminate ideas of artists.

UP 1967/68 saw the emergence of new art magazines looking at the art world from yet another angle: Parkett

(Switzerland), ArtForum (USA), Flashart (Italy), are some of the internationally leading art publications (still) today. Interview was started in 1969 and quickly became part of popular culture.

Are there other independent art magazines that you appreciate out there (apart from VERY, thanks)?

SW Smaller artist magazines have a tendency to come and go after a few issues. The subversive "Rat Catcher," "Frameworks" and "Analytical Art" I liked very much, they were all UK-based and from the early '70s. "Inventory" is a recent one and still going.

UP Over the (almost) 40 years of its (16) publications, Control has changed only slightly in format (from larger to A4), stayed the same in type of contents but varied in the forms of expressions and matters expressed.

SW The first issue was a bit more like a conceptual artwork itself. When I started Control, we were caught in the middle of '60s ideas of modernism and simultaneously preparing for the '70s. Control went through a period of explanation in the '70s: cybernetics, information theory, art practice.... In the '80s it reflected the feeling of an artwork again, visual statements, with a text base. Artists like Anish Kapoor, Bill Woodrow, Tony Cragg, Tony Bevan were contributing.

The '90s started to deal with issues akin to the '70s again. But the language had changed. If you look at the texts of the '70s, they are sometimes barely readable, even unreadable, questioning the meaning of meaning, all the fundamentals. In the '90s the ways of message transmission had changed through the visual age of the '80s.

UP Ideas of consumption, marketing, packaging, global faster living and budding new technology had entered our lives.

SW I think the '90s saw a gradual gulf developing between —as well as a parallel existence of - the obvious commercial system and a more "aware" approach. People start again to look at art for different reasons, experimental ones. Outside the marketplace practice, there are people concerned with educational, social and psychological and community issues.

UP Talking about "interdisciplinary practice" and a "questioning of the system," sounds very familiar to me. The '60s in that respect sound rather close in nature to what we have been experiencing lately. At the same time the upsurge of magazines in the '60s and the one in the late '90s are another parallel.

SW It's 40 years since the '60s and at the time we maybe were looking for expressing individualism. Coming from a more structured society we had to first create a system that allowed for it. Philosophy then was in advance of technology.

Philosophy went quiet through the '80s. In the '90s, technology leapt forward, containing its own ideological message and shaping the world. Today I feel we are more connected to the '60s than any time since, exchanging formal structures with methods of self-organization and mutuality. Today the quest for individuality and self-expression is taken for granted. To characterize the societal situation of today, I would describe it as "informal networks in casuality."

An idea that for me was originated with the first issue of Control, is the idea of contextualization.
"A local, individual truths model of culture, pluralistic rather than centralized."

— A local, individual truths model of culture, pluralistic rather than centralized."—
Stephen Willats

Looking back with the distance of time we discover patterns that were impossible to recognize as they were happening right in front of our eyes. When will our western civilization start to appreciate age and history?

Living in the United States today, I feel caught in an age of perpetual youth culture, and the rest of the world seems to happily follow suit. A whole society celebrating a mental/emotional adolescence in which life doesn't seem to extend past the next day of school. In which everything is about immediate reward and no remorse.

While we are talking, Stephen is actually melting in a London heatwave that hits 90 degrees in the shade. He is dripping, wishing for an in-house pool rather than a mews house from which there is no escape. Myself, I am enjoying the most perfect summer day with a bit of a breeze in the normally unbearable humid concrete jungle of a New York July.

Something is wrong with this picture—although London's Ozone layer has been notoriously hole-ridden. Ten years ago I remember the sun getting stronger in the U.K. People were so unprepared. The daily reports from Brighton beach showed painful strings of sunbathers strongly resembling sausages one had forgotten to turn. One side pale white, the other blistering, burnt. No joke. About six years ago I heard the first radio sun-alert for Hyde Park on a beautiful June day: "Ozone danger alarm! Do not stay in the sun for more than 20 minutes. Please take precautions…" If Stephen is saying that he knows people actually concerned as much with their communities as their careers, I can only hope they have some friends.

Time will tell. In the meantime, this discussion leads to further thoughts. Ape became man through the use of tools. In evolution, this was the beginning of the deadly chase: man vs technology. Who furthers whom, the chicken, the egg. In terms of magazines, what came first? And how did it happen?

I ask my friend Christoph Schifferli, artist books and photography collector. We have a brisk skip through the last century of magazines, looking for hints.

The first artist periodical he recalls is *La Revue Blanche* (1891-1903), an influential literary and artistic journal published by the brothers Natanson in Paris at the wake of the 20th century. Both privately and through *La Revue Blanche*, the publishers were generous supporters of contemporary artists and the arts. Beautifully made, these publications included lino cuts, etchings, wood cuts of avant-garde artists including Lautrec, Bonnard, Vuillard. Among the writers were France's Zola, Gide, Proust and Mallarmé, still relatively unknown at the time. *La Revue Blanche* published Gauguin's manuscript *NoaNoa* as well as translations of Tolstoy, Chekhov, Ibsen, Kipling, Wilde and Twain.

1910 sees the creation of "Der Sturm" (German: "The Storm," 1910-1932). Publisher Herwarth Walden opened a gallery under the same name in 1912 and ran a parallel program in both: works by *Die Brücke, Der Blaue Reiter*, the magazine translated the Futurist Manifesto, an explanation of Orphism by Delaunay and Loos' essays on modern architecture. In 1913 Walden organized the first German Herbstsalon (Autumn Salon), creating an equivalent to the French Salon d'Automne.

In 1917 *Das Kunstblatt* is launched in Germany. GENIUS follows suit as "Zeitschrift für werdende und alte Kunst" "Magazine for current and old art" (1919-1921).

All these, as well as VERVE later in Paris (1937-1958), represented art in its traditional forms of painting, etching and so forth as closely as possible. Most included lithographs as had *La Revue Blanche*, treating the magazine form as a second tier of the creative process.

The moment at which the magazine became a form of expression in its own right was grasped almost simultaneously by a number of different groups: the Dadaists in Paris, the Italian Futurists and Russian avant-gardists in the 1920s all turned against the publication of high-quality reproductions. Instead, they created new works on assembled paper and a new form of magazines emerged: with modest means, they were printed in black and white, in smaller formats, even on news-print, and could resemble political manifestos, even flyers.

After the wars, it is Duchamp in 1945 who earns himself the medal of being the first sole artist to create and design his magazine, VIEW, entirely autonomously, ringing in a new era, a new point of view.

Visuelle Poésie combined images with text/poetry in the '50s but it was Fluxus that adopted periodical publications as a central form of artist activity. Assembled boxes, collages, "objets composés" could be seen simultaneously as periodical or multiple. The format lent itself perfectly to the collaborative group spirit: the publications were cumulative art pieces allowing the contributions of changing Fluxus members.

ANNO I. N. II - FIRENZE, 1 DICEMBRE 1916 - Anno II. L. a. 15 d'ogni mese - Redazione Via Brunelleschi, 9 FIRENZE - Amministrazione Stab. Grafici Martini Prato Toscano Abb. Annuo L. 2,50 - Ogni numero Cent. 10

L'ITALIA "FUTURISTA

DIREZIONE ARTISTICA

BRUNO CORRA - E. SETTIMELLI

Gloria all'italiano Guido Guidi che su apparecchio italiano ha battuto il record mondiale d'altezza (7950 m.)

GUIDO GUIDI

mots en liberté

parole in libertà di *Marinetti*

Niente di TEDESCO

F. T. MARINETTI
FUTURISTA

ZEITSCHRIFT
FÜR ALLES
REVIEW FOR
EVERYTHING
TÍMARIT
FYRIR ALLT
9

Paralleled in the United States was this group by SMS (Shit Must Stop 1968-1969). Initiated by the painter William Copley, SMS produced in total six sets of small precious boxes containing objects like screenprints, records. Participants included Lichtenstein, Nauman, Ono, Weiner, Roth. Beuys became involved in Interfunktionen (1968-1972).

Dieter Roth then proposed yet another outlook with his magazine *Review of Everything* in 1975. The Canadian artist group General Idea published FILE (1972-89), mimicking the look of LIFE magazine, famously prompting a much-publicized lawsuit from the Time-Warner corporation.

162

7

FILE

MAY JUNE , 1972

IL CAPPELLO RIPRODUCE I PARTICO-
LARI DI UN ABITO DI JEAN-PAUL GAUL-
TIER POUR GIBÒ.

DA MILANO, PARIGI E LONDRA, TUTTE LE TENDENZE DEL PRET-
A-PORTER FEMMINILE PER LA PRIMAVERA-ESTATE: UN'INEDITA
LETTURA DELLE PROPORZIONI OFFRE STRAORDINARIE SOR-
PRESE ● DA NEW YORK: ARTE E FILOSOFIA DEL SUCCESSO IN
STILE XIX SECOLO PER DAVID MC DERMOTT E PETER MC GOUGH

From a man-against machine point of view, we can see three main moments in this 21st century of [magazine] publication. The '20s offered a democratization of print, which was used by artists just as it was by the polit machinery parallel to radio, ringing in the beginnings of mass communication. Technology was pushed to many new levels through the wars.

After the reconstruction of the '50s, the '60s combined a number of elements: a necessary redefinition of values based in a new postwar society—a strengthened cultural morale of the United States which, shaking off some history and traditional (European) values, began to blend high and low culture. New techniques made possible and celebrated industrial reproduction in manufacturing as well as in art.

The '90s saw a rapid development of the micro-chip technology, enabling larger entities to have maximum control, however equally allowing the individual to operate much more independently. There used to be first/second/third worlds, colonies and commonwealth, industrial countries and developing countries. In 2001 the difference is the "digital divide." Media comm- unication means market vote, means power and the sustaining of power.

Courtesy: François Berthoud

At the beginning of the new millennium the right to individuality in our society is taken as a natural right. However, what does that mean? "Being individual?" What can we define ourselves with, offset ourselves against, even rebel against if all—acceptable—forms are labelled, marketed. With the fall of the wall, decline of "the other" ideology, there are no obvious choices, rights or wrongs. Only cool and uncool. You are "with" or "not with," " in" or "not in" with certain groups. No obvious enemy. Just ourselves, constituting a slow creepy-crawly danger in our own self destruction, which tends to go largely ignored in view of more immediate financial gains or losses. What now. A

pastiche society. Teenagers wearing "Baader-Meinhof" T-shirts, "punks" with $500 hairdos, people watching Pearl Harbour without any previous knowledge of the event. A mayhem of no belief. Everything is possible but no reason to do anything, is there?

All we can do is a little bit ourselves, create our own individual truth. Alone, or within a group. How better than with a magazine?

For their contributions to this article I would like to thank: Christoph Schifferli, Stephen Willats, Max Schumann, Printed Matter, Sarah Shatz, Shannon Kennedy, Mark Dagley, Peter Wang

Ian Skedd

Four proposals for Living Units

*An Exhibition curated by Trapp at the Trylowsky Gallery, Vancouver
for* Inside Magazines

Living Unit #3

Ref.

Ref.

designed & published by synchro design tokyo.

e-mail synchro@bea.hi-ho.ne.jp.

*SPECIAL EDIT.
40pages on 10pages

THE FASHION MADE BY MUSIC.

audience of BRIAN SETZER ORCHESTRA
photography by Yuichiro TAMURA

174

audience of THE MARCH OF MODS
photography by Hiroki OBARA

audience of R-NIGHT
photography by Daisuke AKITA

audience of NUMBER GIRL
photography by P.M.KEN

audience of MARYLIN MANSON
photography by Teiko TSUJIMOTO

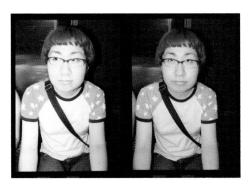 

179

audience of POLYSICS photography by Tomoko KANEUCHI
audience of NUMBER GIRL, D.M.B.Q, QURULI photography by Tomoko KANEUCHI

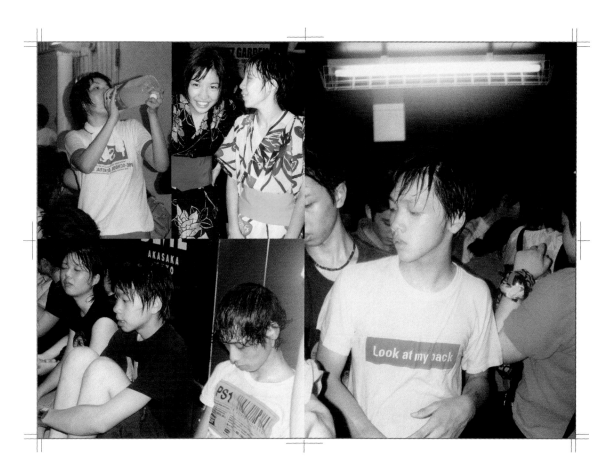

audience of PRE-SCHOOL
photography by Tomoko KANEUCHI

WHAT ARE YOU LISTENING NOW?

CAPSULE GIANTS

HI-STANDARD

INSTANT CYTRON

モーニング娘。

PORT OF NOTES

BON JOVI

IMAJUKU

HI-STANDARD

BEN HARPER

HIPHOP (MIXED BY HIMSELF)

BUDDHA BRAND

MAD CAPSULE MARKETS

SNAIL RAMP

HIPHOP (MIXED BY HERSELF)

WHAT ARE YOU LISTENING NOW?

SILVA

THE BLUE HEARTS

4D JAM (MIXED BY HIMSELF)

MONEY MARK

椎名 林檎

SNAIL RAMP

ENVY

STAIND

SLIME

MINA

OBLIVION DUST

BECK

WILD HEARTS

中山美穂

2 PAC

WHAT ARE YOU LISTENING NOW?
(Reseach on the street)

audience of THE FUJI ROCK FESTIVAL 00 photography by Yuichiro TAMURA, Takayo AKIYAMA
audience of UNKNOWN RAVE PARTY photography by ATZUO

Brian Jungen

Prototype for New Understanding, #5 and #6

Sec.

Sec.09

Sec.09 Summer/Fall 2001 - the sports issue Lard Buurman, atelier puckie (Uta Eisenreich & Suska Mackert), Judith van Eijken, Marie Jose Jongerius, Melle Hammer, Selina Houwing, Frank Kok, Wieteke de Lange, Ian Lopez, Laurence and Philippe from Switzerland, Floor Koomen, Rogier Maaskant, Dorothé Meyer, Martien Mulder, Viviane Sassen, Maurice Scheltens, Martine Stig, Johannes Schwartz, Alex Trüb (Kronos design), Annelys de Vet, Harry de Weijer, Henk Wildschut and Raymond Wouda.

Sec. has started from the idea of creating a space for autonomous work by various artists. It should be considered as a collection of personal images, that was created without any commercial purpose. Sec. welcomes all suggestions and participation. You can send your images/ideas (please only recent or unpublished work) as follows: Send colorcopies at A4 - size (maximum). We will ask for the originals if necessary. Put name / address / phone number and all credits on the back of every copy. Any introduction / information about the work is welcome. Send it to: **Sec.** Singel 370 sous. 1016 AH Amsterdam the Netherlands. T +31 (0)20 6823211 E sec@singel370.nl

Editiorial staff for the sports issue Yolanda Huntelaar, Roosje Klap, Martien Mulder, Richard Niessen, Martine Stig, Viviane Sassen **Design** Roosje Klap

this is asianpunkboy world...

matter

seam

ovulate

dissent

reduction

lust

oxidation

caramel

meter

singular

bending

kinesic

breathe

somnolent

hurried

pluck

mesozoic

fraternity

hurricanes

hyphens

intimacy

immensity

approach

solidifying

shell

luminous

eventless

extension

weld

syntax

ontological

fixation

steam

metaphysician

tissue

occasion

agglutination

conscious

wardrobes

phenomenologist

autonomy

debaptising

polarity

irrationality

convenient

construct

cosmicity

restfulness

vicariously

pressure

nucleized

corners

faithlessness

shell-dog

perceptible

bachelard

imparting

pupils

diastole

chariot

realities

becomes

plateau

ultra-hearing

hallucinations

erudite

denegation

characterological

non-house

asianpunkboy: the empty city

Re-

• Letter

Re-Magazine
Prinsengracht 397 sous
1016 HL Amsterdam
The Netherlands
T 00. 31. 20. 3209032
E mail@re-magazine.com

Charles H. Scott Gallery
Emily Carr Institute of Art and Design
Vancouver British Columbia V6H 3R9

re: 01/022 text RE- in

Amsterdam August 7th, 2001

Hi Patrik and Judith

Here's the handwritten schoolgirl txt plus credits and intro. We'll send you the cover by Fed Ex asa its finished.
Can't wait to see the book!

Julia

A Re-magazine contribution by Lernert Engelberts, Julia van Mourik, Jop van Bennekom and Arnoud Holleman.

Astrid is 12 years old and a first year secondary school pupil in Hilversum. She is the youngest sister of Jop
van Bennekom, Re-Magazine's editor in chief. For English class she has been asked to hold a talk in English
on a subject of her own choosing. She chose Re-Magazine.

RE- MAGAZINE

History of Magazines

My lecture of today is about
Re-Magazine.
Since 1700 magazines excist in The
Netherlands, because of new ideas about
the world and the freedom of press a lot
of magazines were published in the
Netherlands. Nowadays there are many
magazines in the shops. I went to the
Bruna in Hilversum and counted 756
different magazines! Re-Magazine is a
magazine that you can also buy in the shop,
but it doesn't look like other magazines.
For example it has a lot of white space
between the text and the photos. It's
everyday life in a magazine.

History of Re-Magazine.

Re-Magazine excists since 1997. It started
as an exam project of my brother Jop at
art school. He wanted to make a magazine
about normal things. Not all the famous and
glossy things you read in real magazines.
At first it was real small, but now, four
years later it has 15000 copies. The first
issues were in Dutch but now it is in
English so everybody can read it. Now
Re-Magazine is made by three men and one

woman, they are called Jop van Bennekom, Lernert Engelberts, Arnoud Holleman and Julia van Mouril. They are 20 and 30 years old. They live in Amsterdam. Also other people write for Re-Magazine, man and woman, also about 30 years old, from all over the world. There are also a lot of photographers.

a visit to the office

I think it is a beautiful magazine. It looks really nice, it is printed on glossy paper, but I don't understand most of it. I mean, normally in a magazine you see a lot of pictures of popgroups for example, but in Re-Magazine there are a lot of strange pictures, like a girl kissing a plant and a tree, or a boy with a box over his head. I don't know why people make pictures like that and then I asked my brother and he told me that it was too complicated to explain.
Especially for this lecture I payed a visit to the Re-Studio in Amsterdam. It was the first time I went alone by train. It took me half an hour and Jop picked me up at the Central Station which was really big with a lot of people with bags going rapidly somewhere. I thought the office would be very busy. Like you see on television. You know, people typing on computers and all kinds of people walking in and out, but there were only four people

in the office. The room was really hot but they didn't open the window 'cause then they couldn't work off all the noises of trains passing by. I asked Jop what he was doing. He told me that he was writing an article about a spot on the office-wall. He explained that he wanted to give words to small and insignificant things. Insignificant means when something is not so meaningfull. The things you normally don't see or think about. This is the theme for the coming issue. Jop also told me that he makes a magazine because in that way he can talk back in the stream of media that falls over you every day. I think that it is a nice thought. I mean, I sometimes too get lost in all possibilities. When I was ten I wanted to be an actrice, but now I think I want to be nothing really. I don't know.

An editor is someone who types the text. I asked Arnoud and Lernert how they make the magazine. They told me that first they type some texts about things they want to type about and than they give it to each other and the others can add or take away things from the text untill everybody thinks it's okay. Then they ask a photographer to make a photo that fits and then Jop does the design and than it goes to the printer where they make copies of it and then there are a lot of Re-Magazines. The printer puts them in boxes and brings them to the publisher.

The publishers put them in the plane to distributors in other countries, they bring the magazines to the shop, where you can buy one. You can buy it in London, Paris, Berlin, Antwerp, Stockholm, Zürich, Tokyo, Seoul. Taipei, Sydney, Vancouver, New York, Los Angeles and San Francisco. These are places I've never been. You can also order on the internet, then the publisher doesn't need to put the boxes in the plane, then the magazine is directly send to you. You can also subscribe, then the magazine is send to you three times a year.

Interview with editor Julia

1. Since when does Re- Magazine excist ?
 - 1997, 4 years.
2. Is it going well with Re- Magazine ?
 - Yes.
3. How many pages is Re- Magazine ?
 - 84 pages.
4. How many words are there in Re-Magazine ?
 - about 30.000 words.
5. How many pictures ?
 - 52
6. How many people work for Re- Magazine ?
 - three men and one woman.
7. Is it nice to work for Re- Magazine ?
 - Yes very nice, sometimes not.

about issues

The theme of one of the issues of
Re-Magazine was boring. On the cover
was a boy with a piece of tape on his ~~ace~~
nose which made him look like a pig.
Inside it looked like somebody scrathed all
over with a pen. at first you think : how
did that happen? But then you see its
really printed. J really liked it. My best
friend Carla and J are always bored to tears
here in Hilversum. We used to have this
hidden place in this old gardenhouse at my
place but this is removed 'cause my mother
thought it was dangerous. Now we always
hang around behind the garage of Carla's
father.
a few issues back there was this coverpicture
of an old woman. J think it's good that there
are not only young skinny women on the
cover of magazines, you can get anorexia from
that. anorexia is a dangerous disease. You
don't want to eat and you think you are
fat although you are really skinny. You
can't look at yourself normally and you hate
yourself. This old woman on the cover used
to be an photomodel years ago and she
really looked like the mother of Carla. J
showed the picture to the mother of Carla
and she thought it looked like here as well.
Carla's mother read the magazine and told
me it was about reconnect yourself.

Making contact again with the world, with
your neighbours, with your family. I don't
see Jop very often. I regret that, but Jop
is really busy. Once a month he visits us on
Sunday. Most of the time he doesn't speak
about his work. My mother askes him about
it, but most of the times he gets irritated
when he thinks she doesn't understand him.
She thinks a magazine should contain
information about the lenght of the skirt,
recipies and make-up tips. My mother thinks
it is very admirable that Re-Magazine can
make something about nothing.

Casey McKinney

L.A.
Independent

(coverless) mini-mag by Casey McKinney

Photo 2001 by Dave Muller

I have struggled for a while with how to approach the ten pages that I have been allotted and have wasted a lot of time in doubt and vacillation. I set out with a plan to write an essay on Los Angeles based independent magazines, concentrating on those that have had an influence on me personally, while seeking out others of a kindred spirit, both contemporaneous and from recent history. At this stage in the game (four days from the deadline), however, I am throwing my hands up, pleading ignorance, abandoning the essay format for a kind of apologetics. Not from a dearth of information, mind you, but from a surprising abundance.

Los Angeles, compared to its two urban rivals, New York and San Francisco, has relatively few publications or publishing houses. From my experience, it's not exactly the place to be if you're looking for a job as an editor or staff writer. Writers get paid little enough as it is, and if interning at *Flaunt* is—well—if that's the way to get work here, then I say fuck it, make your own magazine. Get out the carpetbag and pay the bills freelancing or do something else entirely. Most of the major publications presently operating in LA are pretty lousy. Not to name names, but *Detour, Flaunt, Los Angeles Magazine* (whoops sorry I am naming names)—*come on* ?

But that's not to say that things have always been this way. When you talk to someone who has lived here for a while, like punk pundit, author and archivist Brendan Mullen, you glean a sincere reverie for some of LA's deceased publications. Magazines like *Nomagazine, Slash, Wet* (the Magazine of Gourmet Bathing), *Lobotomy, Backdoorman, Egozine, Scratch, Bomp, Ben is Dead*, and many others of a more independent nature were all born, bred and buried here in LA. All, I assume, had their bombastic first issue manifestos, their in and out of house quarrels, their days of being the underdog, the days careening towards the establishment, and the days of little relevance or readership. Of course I don't know, as I'm not a native to this town and am probably too young to have an opinion if I was. Dead magazines. Everyone has a favorite.

Unfortunately for all that have to read these ten pages, I must go ahead and say, I did a seven page interview with Raymond Pettibon so that leaves me with very little room to write about things that I know nothing about, thankfully. *See how a sentence can meander from "unfortunately" to "thankfully." That's the sign of a gifted wordsmith!*

But seriously, I had revelations looking through these old magazines. Like Hamlet fondling the skull of Yorick, I sensed that soon enough my magazines will be old magazines, dead magazines, just as I and everyone else will be dead one day as well (how profound). A little mortality trip. And the dead deserve much respect. Here's to *Wet* magazine for introducing Ecstacy to the world 20 years before *Time*. Here's to the critic from *Bomp* who thought Tom Petty was a punk rocker! Here's to *Scratch* and their fusion of hair rock, punk rock and Melrose gossip, years before the name Spelling meant dumbass blonde (who was quite good incidentally in that movie with Parker Posey)! Here's to Bill Dakota and the Hollywood Star for revealing that Marlon Brando not only liked to have girls stick fingers up his ass, but for guys to suck his cock as well! Here's to *Slash* for dissing Phonograph Record magazine. Here's to *Flipside* and *Lobotomy* for giving the finger to *Slash*. Here's to *Nomagazine* for trying to be artsy. And here's to *Egozine* for trying too hard to be artsy and in retrospect succeeding.

Lastly here's to all the magazines who are still very much alive and in this survey. I respect what you are doing, and though I may jab here and there (Jeff Rian, Jesse Pearson), if you ever want to pay me tons of money to help you guys out, I'd probably consider it.

Some of my favorite Los Angeles publications, not in any order. From left to right: 1) **Ruh Roh**, the now legendary single issue art/text/comic zine from 1992, edited by Mark Ewart and Mitchell Watkins, featuring a huge list of notable folks like Kathy Acker, Charles Ray, Mike Kelly and William Burroughs. If you find one of these, hang on to it. Dave Muller told me that the Charles Ray picture in the magazine, which was commissioned just for *Ruh Roh,* recently sold for something like $350,000. What that means for the value of the zine, I have no idea, but I imagine at least a couple of bucks. 2) **Snowflake** existed for three issues, and was published seasonally (you skiers know what that means) from 1996 to 1998. Snowflake is one of the reasons I decided to make a magazine. I had never seen anything like it before. Brainchild of Benjamin Weissman and Lisa Anne Auerbach, it was an obsessive meditation on a cold and fluffy form of precipitation, which featured stories, poems, sermons, porn, meatloaf recipes, ski reports, upskirts, the best classifieds you have ever seen, and the best graphic design you have ever seen (thanks to Gail Swanlund, whose b & w typographical wizardry can make you forget what color is). Plus it featured LA's best artists (like all of them and about 90% of them ski...weird?) and writers along with friends, family and some of Ben's students. Equally the quotidian and the sublime, proof of LA's strong sense of artistic community, and a quasi-religious experience to boot, there will never be another magazine like it. 3) & 4) **Goth Slut** and **Pee Stories** are two zines by Matthew Greene. Matt did a good deal of the design on *Animal Stories*, and I owe everything I know about computers to him. When he's not designing spaceships for tv commercials, he's a photographer, a sculptor and a maker of zines like these. *Pee Stories*, in the tradition of *Snowflake*, is a meditation on a single theme. If you think about it, you pee several times a day, and over a lifetime, if you don't get at least one or two good stories out of it all, then, damn I don't know what to say...go back to bed. And when you go to bed, take a copy of *Goth Slut* with you. That is if you're into dead looking girls dressed in black. Matt has been archiving images of these girls and their black poetry from the Internet for some time now. He edits the poetry down to the basics, focusing on words like reality, darkness, funereal… And in the grainy format of Xerox, the blackness is almost overwhelming. 5) **Enigmatic Militant Asian Christian Teen**?   6) **American Homebody** is another zine from Lisa Anne Auerbach. Though it has recently gone online (http://www.americanhomebody.com), it is still a formidable alternative to magazines like Living and Good Housekeeping. 6) **Glamour Pussy** is one of Trinie Dalton's many mini-pubs. She's a wickedly good writer and kind of an expert on zines, having maintained the voluminous archive at Beyond Baroque for some time. Her journals have included a Beck Dream Journal, a Unicornucopia fanzine (she's in a band by the same name. All of the songs are about unicorns), and the soon to be released Rodentia, a funny, thorough and insightful ode to a hated order of mammals. 7) **Sad Magazine** is the product of the ever elusive, hermetic I imagine, publisher Mary Burt. Mary helped distribute *Animal Stories* through the MOCA store where she works and soon let on about her amazing zine. Sometimes it's nice to be sad. 8) Last but not least, **Little Caesar** by Dennis Cooper (please see insert in the Pettibon interview). As I have said before, I'm not a native to LA, but have lived here briefly a couple of times in the past. I took a writing class from Dennis back in '92 and he soon became a friend and mentor. I owe him more than I can say. In 1976 he (and one time co-editor Jim Glaeser) started this magazine with a Rimbaudian enthusiasm for the destruction of the geriatric literary scene that held sway at the time. Cooper's magazine, which began with a sweet, naïve, yet earnest premise (see insert again), soon evolved into a heroic literary journal, featuring the likes of Allen Ginsberg, Warhol everyman and Velvets whipcracker Gerard Melanga, along with Lou Reed and other Velvets, Joe Brainard, Amy Gerstler and Eileen Myles. *Little Caesar* was the fulcrum of a revolutionary literary art movement in Los Angeles in the late '70s, and many who first appeared there are still setting the pace today.

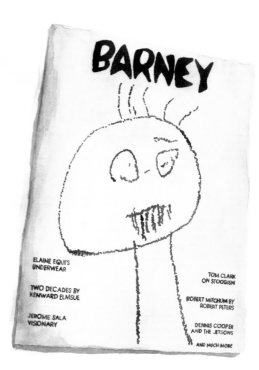

Clockwise from top left: *Little Caser, Lobotomy, Barney, Flipside.* All 2001 by Dave Muller, courtesy of the artist and Blum and Poe.

A conversation with artist and independent magazine publisher
Raymond Pettibon

7/19/2001

Me: I wanted to write about you in this article that I am doing for a book on independent magazines. When I talked to Lisa I was just going to see about getting repros, but she mentioned that maybe I should talk to you. To be honest it makes me really nervous to talk to you because you are one of my favorite artists. So would that be cool to ask you some questions about your early zines and publishing?

Pettibon: Yeah.

M: How did you come up with the idea of making zines? I mean was it just a matter of getting the work out there? I read that it was right after college that you did your first *Tripping Corpse*.

P: Yeah. I guess the first one wasn't *Tripping Corpse*. It was a book called *Captive Chains* and that was 1978. I think the first *Tripping Corpse* was maybe a few years later. So I guess one would have been '77-'78 and the other would have been like '80-'81.

M: So *Captive Chains* was right after college and you were an economics major?

P: Yeah.

M: Did you take art classes in high school or was that something that you just developed on your own?

P: I think maybe one, an art history class but I didn't actually... I mean I think I withdrew in the 1st week or two. No I don't have an art background as far as schooling goes.

M: But you have always drawn since you were young, right?

P: Oh yeah.

M: Were you intending on going into a career in something with your economics degree and then you just decided not to?

P: Actually, I mean as far as... when you're that young... most people have... I mean I guess some people have a very defined sense of direction and mine was... I wouldn't say it was particularly nebulous, but it wasn't... what happened was I (pause)...I got interested in economics when I was about 13, 14, 15 years old and that continued on until my first

few years in college and by that time—by the time I had already declared a major and was committed to that one field or discipline rather than another—I had already lost interest. And for a number of reasons. The politics of the day and so forth. My world historical view of economics was very extreme in those days. I mean now it's very commonplace. UCLA at the time was and still is I suppose a very free market, radical... I wouldn't say it's left or right, but where the left and the right meet. And since I've been

Both images on this page from *Tripping Corpse* 4 by Raymond Pettibon, 1984. Courtesy Regen Projects.

an anarchist philosophically... I mean my political, economic viewpoint...

M: Do you consider yourself a libertarian then?

P: (pause) Uh...pretty much. I mean I'm not card carrying one way or another.

M: So when you joke in the books in a fake interview with Mike Watt, and you have him saying how far Right you are, in regards to his political views, there is some truth to that then, right?

P: Well let me... I'm trying to think of what you are talking about there. That was a fake interview with Watt in one of the *Tripping Corpses*? About politics?

M: Yeah you made kind of a caricature of his left wing politics, and then in the end you reveal yourself through one of your questions, something about family and pre-marital sex, and he's like "Oh it's Pettibon!"—and it was supposed to be somebody else doing the interview.

P: Oh, ok, yeah.

M: The setup kind of reminded me of one of the Spy vs. Spy segments from *Mad* magazine...

P: Yeah, ok. I vaguely recall that. Yeah Mike is... I don't want to put words in his mouth. He's um (long pause). He... Let's put it this way. In 1977 that kind of... there's been a big displacement of... within at least the academic community, between that kind of staunch Marxism and radical... in other words, when I was 15, I was on the extreme end of... I was pretty radical. Now it's become commonplace and I don't, you know there's, aside from... there's still plenty of (long pause)... kind of Marxist um... that was commonplace in 1977 that is still around, but it's in like maybe... you actually have to go to, I mean not even art, but maybe sociology, or... you know Marx and Freud and...

M: So you were maybe trying to unveil the myth of that—the whole utopian hippie thing. Is that what you mean?

P: No, I know what you mean, but that wasn't... I never saw myself as this... It wasn't about pointing fingers and trying to convince people. It wasn't didactic. My videos and my art, which is what you are probably thinking of—around that time, in the punk years when I was doing stuff about hippies and '60s politics—it was just comedy. But on the other hand, in the mid to late '70s there still was this really degraded form of '60s people involved in journalism and art, and it had just become so farcical by that time. Punk eventually went the same way as well, in my opinion, but it was much more marginalized. So it wasn't really... I mean the '60s were... they were supposed to take over the world.

M: So when you first started your magazines… I'm trying to figure out the impetus. Like I said, was it mainly just to get your art out there? I mean doing stuff for your brother's band Black Flag and the other SST bands that you did art for, the album covers, flyers… I mean I've read that you've said it wasn't about the music, only the art. Could you elaborate maybe on how you came to do your art that way? I mean did you think that one day you would be showing in galleries, or was it more that at the time you weren't really thinking about that, and you were pumping out the work so you just put it together?

P: I mean it wasn't one or the other. I assumed, although you can't really assume, in my case anyway… I don't have the kind of personal psychology where… I mean I never count on anything happening until it does, or even long after that. I mean it wasn't about the music, but then I get asked these kinds of questions all the time and I get kind of cajoled into accepting or betraying one thing or another. I mean art isn't music. I don't make notes on guitar or bass and that work wasn't illustrating the music. It wasn't commercial art that is. I don't know what to say beyond that.

M: Well I'm only twenty-eight myself and that's how I first came across your art. When I was kid, buying Black Flag records and Minutemen records and of course Sonic Youth… I think I was subconsciously influenced by your album cover art in terms of my own artistic endeavors. I was more interested in art at that age and later got into writing. When I drew, I would copy album covers, the graphics and symbols from punk records.

P: Well I think in the same way I had a lot of roundabout influences and inspiration through music as well. Without question a lot of people in art and beyond were influenced by what was happening. I mean even in the '60s, which my art kind of turned against or digressed—I mean it wasn't my generation—but on the other hand there was a lot of affection with that. And then punk, the Ramones, Stooges, Black Flag. I mean of course that had something to do with my work. I've kind of lost my train of thought. What was your original question?

M: I guess I'm trying to… I mean I make magazines myself and… I mean I wanted to try and make a magazine that was like a real magazine, but done from home without any advertising or anything. Which is a really hard thing to do, to make viable. I probably lose at least a dollar or two on each magazine. But I do it just to do it, and to get my friends exposure and… I guess it was in *Captive Chains* you were talking about why you were getting into it, and you joked that it was for "THE

MONEY," but I was seriously wondering—did you plan it out so that, I mean I noticed that the books were priced $1.25, $1.75, $1.50, etc, variable prices. I was just wondering if you worked it out so that you were at least breaking even. I know that's a stupid question.

P: No it's not a stupid question, but… those books were… going back to economics… those books were so far out of the marketplace that supply and demand and pricing was irrelevant. And that's why it became… Ok, well actually the first one was 5,000 copies.

M: Wow that's a lot.

P: Yeah of course. But at that time, unless you… nowadays there are other ways of printing… but at that time you either had to

From New Wavy Gravy 2 by Raymond Pettibon, 1985 By Raymond Pettibon. Courtesy of Regen Projects

print that much or… I mean to print a few hundred copies it would cost just as much.

M: And you did that offset?

P: Yeah, it was offset and if you did the accounting for it, it was probably the only one that made money. Actually I don't even know about that. But I know the other ones didn't. The other ones for a while were 500 copies, which were I think offset as well. And then there were the Xeroxed ones, usually 50 copies, or even less, 30 to 50 copies, or 60, or 75 copies, sometimes even a few hundred. But usually the larger editions, the 500 ones, I threw away most of those, so the print runs were kind of in the neighborhood of 35 to

maybe 150 or 200. And obviously they weren't about making money or breaking even.

M: Did they get you other graphics jobs?

P: No, I've never done commercial art. I mean I've done record covers, and to this day if someone asked me to do a record cover I'd do it, but very rarely do I ever get paid for it. The reason behind it was it to—if you write or make art—it's about communication, getting your work out there, at least theoretically. I mean I have always had a vague, nebulous idea about who my audience is. It's not something I can really do numbers with. And also beyond that, more than that, it is to have a record of the work so that…

M: Did you have to scale the drawings down or were they drawn at the same scale as the books?

P: In general no, but they weren't a whole lot bigger. If they weren't exact scale, they were maybe two or three times larger.

M: Because you knew the final product would be black and white, did you stick to black and white primarily when you were drawing?

P: Yeah. Um…

M: (interrupt) Oh sorry. Go ahead.

P: No go ahead.

M: Well I was reading in one of the essays, I believe it was the one by Ohrt, in *The Books* book, in which he kept referring back to film noir and its influence on your work—and while I can see that to a degree, I was also wondering if maybe, because you knew of the limitation of working with the black and white format, in order to get the work across more clearly you appropriated expressionistic techniques. Because in reproduction it would make it… I mean I've seen so many zines in which people don't understand that they are working with black and white and that if they don't deal with contrast in the right way, that it's going to look like crap. I was just wondering if maybe the medium and the limitations pushed your work in a certain direction?

P: Yeah, that is probably true. I mean it wasn't like I was compelled or forced to work in black and white in this… well, black and white, very stark contrast to make it print well, but to this day I still consider the printed page to be… I mean I have more in common with that than putting something in a gallery or on museum walls. Which isn't necessarily limiting… I mean with film noir for instance, which by the way is very… I don't know how that keeps coming up with my work. I think that's very overstated. But on the other hand I understand what they're talking about… But let me put it this way, some of the film noir I think at its best came out of the limitations of what they had to deal with—the budget, they only had black and white stock…

M: …yeah, and limited stage props and construction budgets. Like what Welles did with *Citizen Kane*, creating huge spaces by just messing with the lights. Or Caligari, how they painted the shadows. I mean they created that style because otherwise it wouldn't have shown up on camera.

P: Right. Yeah.

M: That was what I wondering with your work. I didn't realize that you went offset at first and then to a Xerox format. With Xerox it's so hard to…

P: But even offset, the way I do it. You can do more with a Xerox but… I mean I don't know how it is now with that kind of thing, but back then if you took in anything that was even like a wash they'd say don't even try. You'd have to do either zipitone or black and white. So in other words it wasn't about style or this kind of precious style… I mean now and then you see these kind of films or even in art or comics whatever, they are kind of like… I mean if you have the technology and the means and the resources to go beyond that then why not, but if you don't then fine. I mean it's the same with recording. Until the last twenty or thirty years there was… Let's put it this way, most of the history of recorded music was done live in the studio, even with full orchestras. There weren't all of these… I mean nowadays any half-ass band has the resources to do all kinds of fiddling around in the studio incessantly. Does that make it necessarily better? That's still something I deal with in my work.

M: Now you still make zines, and so much of your work has this historical distance. I was wondering if you keep up with the new technologies. I mean do you even use the Internet?

P: No I don't but I should. It's kind of like what we were just talking about. I think anyone is cheating themselves if they don't. If they think they are going to do this precious kind of retro thing or figure that it's more pure to film something in black and white or silent, or to record four track or whatever, vinyl is better and so forth, I think no it's not… I don't put a value one way or another, either for or against. The reason I don't do drawings on computers is partly because it's not my generation. I mean you're a lot younger than me and, I don't know, I guess personally, I don't have an aptitude for learning new things as much as some people do.

M: Well it seems like with the volume of work that you do, that you don't have the time.

P: That's part of it as well. It's probably wrongheaded to a degree but I don't know, I don't feel a huge need to do it but…

M: Yeah sometimes I wish I didn't have an Internet account, because I swear it just keeps me from doing work. I mean it's good for doing research, and the other new technologies do allow me to make a full color magazine from home, but I still know relatively little about it all… I mean I still have to get friends to help me. I was also wondering, when you were first making zines, were you keeping up with the other zines that were coming out at the time? Or were there many LA zines coming out at the time? And if you did keep up with any others, are you still a fan? Do you still buy them?

P: Well what kind of zines?

M: I don't know because I've never really been a big fan myself. I feel kind of guilty about it, but I don't really buy other…

P: There weren't…

M: I mean for this article, to represent LA I am talking about you, Dennis Cooper's early magazine *Little Caesar*, Benjamin Weissman's *Snowflake* and that's pretty much it.

P: But that was totally different (*Little Caesar*). That was poetry and fiction and… literature, and mine was kind of this freakish… It didn't have anything to do with… I mean it did have something to do with, comics for instance, although if you looked at the people who were doing comics then they were completely dismissive and disparaging of what I was doing, and you could say the same thing about music magazines. Punk magazines like *Slash* and *Flipside* were very dissmissive as well. All of those were.

M: Were they offended?

P: No, no. That sounds like I am giving myself too much credit. It wasn't in the same universe.

M: So they never even recognized it.

P: No, why would they?

M: I guess what I am wondering is, did you recognize any contemporaries at the time? I mean I know like… who else was doing stuff like that?

P: You would have to… I mean be my guest… you tell me.

M: No, I know. I can't think of anyone really. I mean I would say that prior to that there is some continuity between you and *Crumb*, and I guess in the art world sense, Mike Kelly, Jim Shaw and guys like that, but who was doing… I mean Mike Diana maybe? (dog barking) I'm just trying to think of who was doing…

P: I was a generation or two apart from the '60s underground. I mean there are a few people who I think I got to know later more than at the time—Justin Green and…

M: So there wasn't… I mean punk didn't necessarily spur on… I mean there were definitely a lot of fanzines, but art zines, if you want to call what you were doing an art zine, there wasn't an explosion of that as well?

P: Believe me, and I have always been very generous with my sources and influences, I would be glad to acknowledge anyone who…

M: So after you became more well known, who do you recognize as being in the tradition of what you were doing?

P: It wasn't like there was this complete desert and I was like the light in the wilderness, but at the same time I wouldn't… I mean it's not about one person or me or anything else. I think you could be safe to say that at the time of my formative stages it was very different in that basically, since then, the use of text—text with image is much more commonplace and accepted, compared to then. But then you know, it's not about… I mean originality is not what I am trying to put across here.

M: I guess I am just trying to get a sense of the LA magazine landscape, and maybe I am trying to force a round peg into a square hole…

P: Oh no no…

M: And I want to include you in this survey, which, I mean, I see what you were doing as an independent magazine publisher…

P: Right.

M: And the people that they are including in the survey are like *Purple* and *McSweeney's* and *Index* and stuff like that, and they said well, can you do something LA based? And I'm like ok, so I'll talk to Dennis Cooper, Ben Weissman and maybe I'll see if I can talk to Raymond Pettibon.

P: Ok well, what about *Nomagazine*? Bruce Colberg. Do you know that?

M: Yeah Brendan Mullen gave me a copy of that to scan but I haven't had a chance to look at it much. So that was something that you kept up with and read?

P: He published some of my work. I don't know. Beyond that, it was such a small universe in those days. There really… I mean maybe these things come in cycles. If you look at the sixties, the hippies, and then, well even in the fifties. I think fanzines, if you did a history of that…

M: I don't know, the magazines that they are dealing with in this survey seem to be more like style-based magazines that happen to have a more independent flare to them. And that was why I was kind of surprised when they asked me to be included in the survey, because I feel like my magazines are about as non-fashion based as you can get.

P: What about Mark Gonzales' stuff?

M: Yeah, but I guess he's San Francisco based.

P: Oh this is all LA?

M: Well that's what I told them. I mean do you read magazines? I mean are there some in particular that you keep up with or subscribe to?

P: Like fanzines?

M: Well more like… or maybe fanzines that you like or you see value in?

P: Well this is one of those things that I'll probably remember like a week from now. Like there's this really great fanzine that…

M: Do you buy magazines like *Purple* or *Index* or? Are you interested? Or even *Frieze* or *Artforum*? I mean do you keep up with those?

P: …mmm, not as much as I probably should. You know compared to the era where I started there was such a dearth of… Well now I remember another one. There was *Backdoor mag.*

M: *Backdoorman*?

P: Was it *Backdoorman*? Yeah you know S*lash* and…

M: And you read all of those at the time.

P: Yeah, pretty much.

M: Weren't you doing some journalism too?

P: Me? No.

M: Oh I guess that maybe I was inferring that from one of your skits.

P: Yeah that was probably (laughing)… Don't believe everything that you…

M: Well you taught school for a while right?

P: Well yeah, in the mid eighties I taught junior high and high school and I taught some art school infrequently, but that was about it.

M: Yeah I was thinking about being a substitute next year just to earn some extra cash.

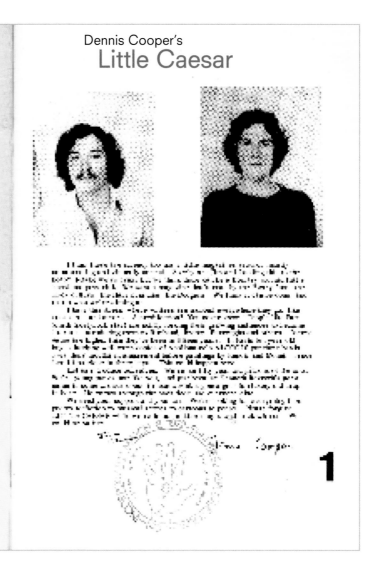

P: Well you know that's probably not a bad idea. Compared to what I was paid back then, it's actually not bad. It's very hard though. Have you taken the CBEST?

M: Yeah I've taken the CBEST. I'm just waiting on my employee number.

P: So are you going to be on the emergency credential?

M: You know I might do that. If somebody offers that to me. But the only drawback is the time factor. I'd be teaching English if I took a full time position, and if I did, I probably wouldn't have time to do anything else—with grading papers and preparing, reading and going to training classes.

P: Well I don't know. It's 90% discipline and 10% teaching. I mean I think the situation has improved some, but it's still very tough, but I wouldn't want to discourage anyone from going into it. I think if you have the time to do that, you should. It'd be worthwhile.

M: Yeah I think if I get offered something I'll take it, but otherwise I'll just sub. Well let's see, continuing… there is something that I have always wanted to ask you about. I have one of your pieces that Dennis Cooper gave me a while back, and it's one of your, I think it's one of your Hawthorne "A" pieces, kind of a test piece for one of those. It's like two red streams that converge with another red stream crossing in the shape of a tilted A, and it says "Dear Me… I have just found the beginning of a letter, which someone had dropped (or a letter of which someone had—should one put it—let it drop): I should rather call it first thoughts for the beginning of a letter; for there are many scratches and corrections (and still it bleeds…). As I cannot use it myself (having got a beginning already of my own) I send it for your use on some great occasion—(Congratulations!)" And then it says, "Perhaps even you recognize its author?" Do you remember that one?

P: Vaguely.

M: I was just wondering what the quote was from or if it was something that you made up yourself.

P: I don't remember all of it, but it sounds like a quote to… Sometimes it's hard to tell that kind of thing over the phone. You have to be more technical. You want to say that again. I mean I might be able to…

M: (repeating)

P: Yeah, no. Offhand I…

M: Yeah it's just that I've had this forever and then finally, looking over these books

that have come out recently, I noticed how many A pieces you have done. I'm just curious. Like I'm a fan of Joyce and I've always been intrigued by the typographical choice of the big S at the beginning of the novel (in early editions). I mean I know that the A in *The Scarlet Letter* means adultery (among other things). But I've always thought that the S from *Ulysses* would make a nice subject for a Pettibon.

P: Well you know like you said, it's based on *The Scarlet Letter*, Hawthorne, but usually if you look at the A drawing letters that I've done, back then the Scarlet A was for adultery, now it's more for AIDS. Like the correspondence between someone who is trying to tell or to intimate to someone… you know that kind of relationship that's kind of up in the air but, or, one way or another… I mean not 100% of the time, but that's usually at least inferred.

M: Yeah I didn't realize. I was thinking more of… I mean I guess you've done stuff with other letters too. I was thinking more about just breaking down the language to just one letter… like Rimbaud's colors of vowels, or just examining what one letter can be. Like A being the first letter in the alphabet, and you mentioned Borges' "Library of Babel" being an influence… And in that story it's related how with the 26 letters of the alphabet, in the almost infinite permutations that they can be arranged, all of the secrets of the universe are contained. And going back to the A, that would be the beginning, the first possibility, sort of a primal singularity. And like with your Va-Voom, the Word speaking.

P: Yeah. No, yea that's… but I tend to be more on the end of the contextual, rather than the formal end of things. So there's usually a…

M: A reference.

P: Yeah. I mean I could never… I'm like the opposite of artists who would put some kind of formal meaning around letters or vowels.

M: But you do see yourself like in the tradition of… well I'm kind of going off the subject, but artists like Blake. Going back to what I was talking about earlier, I was wondering if maybe the medium of the books dictated what you chose as influences and how you go about making your art. Like I was thinking maybe you went back and looked at people who did etchings in the past, or people who did illustrations for books.

P: Well yeah, Blake is really self-evident as someone who did use words and images apart from… in a non-illustrative way. If you go back through the history of, not even book publishing, but in book making or scroll

making or image making there's an illustrative tradition and then there's also an illuminative tradition. And speaking of things like A's or S's or Z's, it becomes calligraphic and part of the design, an ornament as well as… At one time there wasn't a printing press. It was done jot by jot, word by word.

M: Is there a difference between your different script styles that you use? Do you consider those to be different voices or different aspects of yourself? I think I heard someone say that they were different characters. Is that something that has become a system or is that something that just depends on the piece?

P: No, usually it's not, but usually where you see that (different scripts on the same piece) it's because it's done at varying times. I mean in some of those it may be many years between one line and another. That's usually the case. I mean sometimes I may vary it because there may be a kind of internal dialogue with different voices. But that's not usually the case. It could be incumbent on the type of pen that's being used. If it's not the difference in the time, it's probably more likely that.

M: So going back to what we were talking about with the A referring to Hawthorne, but also referring to AIDS, I was thinking of a section from the *Reader*, a Henry James piece from his notebooks where is talking about an idea for a story where he has a person from the American west—Colorado or California, who has all of these European books that he is reads and keeps on his shelf and who likes to keep Europe in his mind that way, but then he is intruded upon by some European who comes to his world and messes with his idea of what he thinks Europe really is. Which obviously I see as… I mean in your work you typically, visually—what is drawn is a contemporary American, or Californian even, subject, suicidal hippies or whatever—on the one end that is, then you have the light, light bulbs, and the bigger themes as well… I mean I was just wondering why it is in particular that you go for like older, European, more circuitous writers in order to deal with current topics…

P: Well I mean James was… even though he renounced his citizenship…

M: Yeah I've always thought of him as a European

P: Yeah, he was always kind of the definition of someone who… like Hemingway… I mean later it became a lot more popular, in the '20s and '30s, a lot of émigrés, Eliot even and Pound, and a lot of his (James') work was based on that theme actually, and Hawthorne as well, but yeah… I know what you mean. It does tend to be a circuitous prose style. That's kind of why I like it. If you look at it… obviously in my case, when I do borrow it, I'm breaking down something into very small pieces and at the same time it can be very circuitous, convoluted, meandering around and you can apply all sorts of possibilities.

M: Well is there is a difference between the European and what he (James) thought of as the Westerner—which he described as being caught up in vulgarity, newspapers, democracies and such? I guess I am trying to paint some sort of picture of LA as far as the publishing world is concerned?

P: The publishing world?

M: Well just what makes LA different compared to say New York or Europe even. I mean I guess let's just keep it in the context of art since your books are art as well as being magazines.

P: Well you know I would love to be able to answer that question, but I don't know if I can without falling into some absurd cliché, which is the way Los Angeles is pigeonholed and explained as far as literature and art. You know honestly, I don't know if I… I mean I don't know if there is a distinction. Usually it comes back to these noir clichés, like Chandler for instance, who—speaking of James and going back and forth—was English and came here. I don't know. I mean that is usually so overstated. I mean I think it's just a convenient journalistic contrivance.

M: Yeah. I just have this idea that a lot of the artists from LA who are big now made it in a kind of grass roots manner, in opposition to say New York, which has been established for so long that it didn't need an upsurge like that. But it seems that back when you were getting started and Dennis was starting Little Caesar, and Beyond Baroque, and Mike Kelly and Chris Burden and all of those people erupted out of more of a sense of… a kind of spirit of… I don't know, like we don't need New York? Or…

P: I don't know.

M: I mean I'm not trying to… I mean I don't have to put this in the interview.

P: No, no. That's a legitimate question and I'll try and answer it the best I can. I mean I don't think that. I think if anything, Los Angeles art and writing… I don't think it… I

mean to speak in those terms like, west coast vs. east coast like it's some kind of rapper war… I mean Mike Kelly's from Michigan and Jim Shaw is from Michigan and most of the New York school of artists are from… well people go to New York because… if it's not the center of the art world… I mean there is no reason why there has to be one center… but it's still a hub where… but on the other hand, for a number of reasons, just the way communication has changed… I mean for many years you had to… geography just doesn't mean as much anymore. I mean we

THE AUTHOR IS A MEDIUM $2
Raymond Pettibon

BONAPARTE HAD PASSED THAT WAY.

SHIFTING AS THE STARS SHIFT

SUPERFLUX PUBS

cover of The Author is The Medium, date unknown, by Raymond Pettibon. Courtesy of Regen Projects

have gotten past the horse carriage and I don't think there has been any competition between LA and New York in a long time. I mean even going back to the '60s. But at the same time it's not regional either. I mean I think San Francisco or some cities have this monkey on their back. In San Francisco's case, they have this obsession with Los Angeles, much more than with New York. Whereas Los Angeles… Yeah there's a little of that, just as it used to be in art… You know finally in the '40s and '50s New York could kind of shut the monkey off its back of France. But I don't know, we're separate but equal, but I don't think we need a

constitutional amendment. I don't think it's an issue and…

M: (laughing)

P: You know me, in my case, and just about everyone I know here who is an artist… I don't think there is this community of artists who trade ideas and make these connections and kind of end up creating this certain style, that's provincial or universal. I just don't see that. I mean I know it's not the case for me, and if you go to any art fair or biennial, you'll see artists from the bushes or from… every cargo cult subscribes to *Artforum*… I mean I don't think this idea of… whether it's innocence or provincialism or regionalism apart from the big bad (unclear) of the art world or the media. It's pretty unlikely nowadays for better or worse.

M: I'm just trying to think if there is anything more about magazines that I could ask. I mean I assume you aren't very much swayed by trends in fashion.

P: If you could name some… I mean I'm not good at…

M: Well let me see, who are some of the magazines that are going to be in the survey…

P: Well you know, do you know, I mean this hasn't been around for a long time but *The Hollywood Star*? Which was a gossip, newsstand… Bill Dakota? I really loved that. And there's…

M: Well the only magazines that I see coming out of LA right now are magazines like *Detour* and *Flaunt*.

P: Well, so it's like a slick kind of fashion thing, the kind of thing where you have the hot new actor on the cover?

M: Well what do you think of magazines that are coming out like, well, *Purple* for instance, where it's like an art/ literary magazine, but it is also very fashion oriented. I mean I like it more than a lot of magazines and some friends have been in it, but somehow I see it as, I don't know, kind of a slick way of saying Kate Spade is cooler than Gucci. It just seems like there has been this kind of forced marriage between… and I guess it's because of economics. You have to sell ad space to pay the bills. But where is the line drawn between crass commercialism and something that is considered art? I mean is fashion photography really art? Or is it somehow debased by the context?

P: I don't think it necessarily is. I mean I know when, going back to when I was… I mean my generation, the early punk days, the word "sellout" was a big deal… sellout, poser… and amazingly that has become more of an issue now more than ever, and I think unfortunately, because it just reinforces this prevalent slacker ideology, which I think is too bad, because I think it comes from sincere, genuine forces, whatever. But I think it holds a lot of people back. And it's not about making it, you know, or success… You know I've never lived by that and I'm not going to have to apologize for anything either…

M: But you've never done commercial art either or had any ads in your books so…

P: Well that's not even relevant here. I mean we're not even talking about…

M: I know. I just feel that personally I could probably make my magazines viable if I did somehow include advertising, but then I feel like if I did, I would lose control of what the magazines are about.

P: Yeah I think it's possible if there are strings attached, but are there necessarily strings attached?

M: Well I mean I would have to start making decisions, like why do I like this advertiser rather than this one? Like I pick up a copy of *Zoetrope* and there is a big Winston ad on the back. I like *McSweeney's* because I don't have to look at that (and for a bunch of other reasons). I mean I don't want to get on a high horse or anything like *Adbusters* (which I also really respect) but I feel like you do lose something with advertising… I mean after a while you are going to have to start doing articles about fashion or other things that I am not really interested in.

P: Then if there are strings attached then… I mean I'm not in this position. I'm just questioning… I mean a cigarette ad, on the one hand they have so much money, and because of these kind of editorial decisions, they have less venues to throw their money around to, and they want to be hip and… on the other hand smoking is the major cause of death in… but then I don't think that even they are expecting the editorial content to promote their… on the other hand they are trying to, I mean the reason they advertise in certain places is that they want to have this hip quotient.

M: I mean what if the show down at the Santa Monica museum was listed as "Raymond Pettibon, The Book Show, sponsored by Miller Light" and the only way that you got that show was if all your drawings had a little Miller Light sticker at the bottom.

P: Well, you know I wouldn't do it of course. Yeah, well that's what I'm saying. I mean it wouldn't affect the content or work.

M: Well, take a magazine like say *Purple* again. I mean its advertising is very minimal… I don't know. I just think that what has happened is that people who used to get up in arms or offended by certain things are kind of falling into the same traps as everybody else. This kind of slippery acceptance… Artists promoting fashion and…

P: No, I know what you mean. It is something to think about.

M: I mean because, like you, I came from punk roots—although because of my age, it was a more watered down, second hand version—but still, I think that my magazines have similar anarchistic affinities, not wanting to be tied in with larger corporations…

P: Yeah, but you know I have a little more history with that than you and you would be surprised I suppose…

M: At how crass punk actually was?

P: Yeah if you knew the people who… I've heard this same thing over the years and when it really comes down to it it's… you know when it makes a difference and they really need… you know it's, well, you know, whatever, beggars and choosers.

M: Beggers can't be choosers, true. You have to get the thing printed. But that's one of the things that I admire about your work—I mean not the only thing, of course, but I admire the self-sufficiency, from a publishing standpoint.

P: Yeah but that's why my print run is like 35-75 copies on the other hand. You know if you want to be pure, you've got to find the purest audience, and what does that amount to? I mean life is not… I mean in the long run, everyone's dead and… you know there are bigger issues.

M: Yeah it's just something I have to think about. I mean making magazines… I mean my girlfriend just picked up some fashion magazine and the big new thing again for fall is fur. Big Davy Crockett Hats.

P: Right, yeah, well those things go in cycles and it becomes this kind of transgressive, forbidden… you know something as lame as that. Just because of all of these PETA people. This is how we are going to put our foot down and make a statement. I mean who cares? Right? But you know, I would tend to… I guess like a lot of people you know, this is a subject that keeps coming up, but I

would tend to err on the side of… and I'm not making suggestions but…

M: Err on the side of at least getting it done, right?

P: You know a fur ad or a cigarette ad…

M: Because art is separate from politics?

P: No, no, look, everything is politics in some sense. This is just how people draw the lines. They demonize one thing and (pause)… On the one hand if you look at these slick magazines with all of their fashion and alcohol and cigarette advertisements… they don't have much of a spine in any sense. They are just chasing whatever they can make money with.

M: Yeah that's what I am trying to figure out for this piece. Trying to chart some influences and see how I fit into the thing. Did you get a chance to read anything from *Mall Punk*?

P: Yeah, I liked it.

M: Yeah I'm making a new one right now that's going to be called *Ghost Stories*, so if you've got any good material… I mean anything that is tangentially related.

P: Well if you ever want me to do something that would be cool.

M: Is there anything else that you would like to bring into the discussion?

P: I can't think of anything off hand.

M: What show are you preparing for?

P: I have a show at Whitechapel in London in early September, and other than that, early next year, Barcelona.

Raif Adelberg

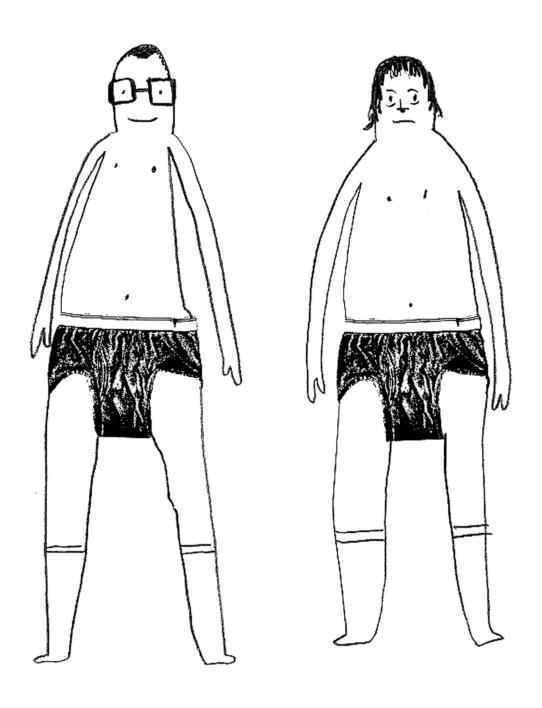

Interviews

By Re- Magazine: *Jop van Bennekom, Leenert Engelberts, Julia van Mourik, Arnoud Holleman*

INTERVIEWS

July 31, 2000

*Interviews by
Jop van Bennekom*

Olivier Zahm of Purple:

Maybe white is favourite color of Purple and design simple and not trendy.

John Kelsey of Made in USA:

Made in USA is made for young ladies of all genders and favourite color is black and white.

Cory Reynolds of Index:

Deep penetration of Index in target group because long interviews in magazine and favourite color is blue.

Gert Jonkers of Butt:

Nobody wants distribution because pink is favourite color of Butt and not much pictures in it.

"Maybe white is favourite color of Purple and design simple and not trendy"

Olivier Zahm of Purple

I am so sorry for inconvenience but I have questions to write you for important interview. Please teach me some answers to questions?

Who are you?
I am Olivier Zahm and editor of Purple and art and fashion critic and bad tennis player.

Why magazine?
A way of continue politics without being militant.

Is magazine good?
It1s best we can, as usual next one will be very best.

What target group magazine?
That difficult question! I know reader profile...between 25 and 45 years old, informed well and part of art and fashion. Purple is not marketed, the readers are result of what we do with magazine. We love to have open circle of readers, more open...

Do magazine penetrate target group?
Yes.

What percentage?
50%?

A lot of pictures in magazine, no? Yes.

A lot of text in magazine, no?
More text now, less pictures.

How old you?
38

How old magazine?
10

You have children, no?
No.

How old children?
I have no children.

Where you live?
Paris, 10th arrondisement.

Address?
9, rue Dupont.

You live alone?
Yes.

You have partners?
Yes.

You have favourite color?
No, yes maybe white.

What is favourite color of magazine?
No purple, purple is pure abstract sign, it1s logo! No meaning symbolic.

You like *Colors*?
I was curious of first issue. I like transnational aspect! But for me magazine

is too mediated, like TV programme.

How edition magazine?
18,000

How real edition?
18,000 is real edition, we claim 30,000.

Why edition?
Very difficult to make just one copy Purple. Too expensive! One copy pays same as two room apartment in Paris!

How much advertisements?
Advertisements pay production costs, scanning, printing, paying text contributions. Photographers not paid yet.

How much one page advertisement in magazine?
$5,000

Who manager advertisement?
Geraldine Postel.

Telephone number?
00.33. 6. 74340131

You good distribution?
Yes, wonderful.

Distribution difficult, no?
Yes, difficult distribution.

You make profit?

No.

How much?
No profit. We are very happy when not loose money.

What is you year income?
$35,000

What year income contributors?
We pay editors, we pay writers for text.

You have Prada?
We have Miu Miu.

How design of magazine?
Design by Japanese art director Makoto.

Why classic design?
Not 'classic design', no. Design simple and not trendy.

Who design?
Makoto with Elein Fleiss.

Address designer?
Tokyo.

Hour rate of designer?
He takes 5 days to do job, that1s around $100... no, $80 a hour.

Magazine made by Apple Mac?
Yes, I mean no.

Which programs?
Purple not designed on computer but with scissors! Makoto designs with real cut and paste. Elein works on computer.

Favourite program of designer?
Quark Xpress.

You have internet?
Yes.

How connection between Apple Mac and edition?
Tools.

Visual change, no?
Not yet! After nineties... no new direction right now.

Visual important, yes?
Less and less.

You competition?
Yes, art competition.

You favourite magazine?
The New Yorker, Vanity Fair.

Why favourite magazine?
To get information from New York.

You are independent magazine?
Yes.

How independent?
Totally.

What is your secret?
I not live in secrets.

What is slogan of magazine?
We never had slogan for Purple. I can make one for you...'Read Gombrowicz
before buying Purple!1

How your slogan?
'Read Gombrowicz!'

"Made in USA is made for young ladies of all genders and favourite color is black and white"

John Kelsey of Made in USA

I am so sorry for inconvenience but I have questions to write you for important interview. Please teach me some answers to questions?

Who are you?
John Kelsey of Made in USA of Bernadebt Corporation.

Why magazine?
It1s really a low budget movie.

Is magazine good?
German man said it was so good he couldn't1t breathe when reading. Then there was bad page and he could breathe again.

What target group magazine?
Three o'clock in the afternoon people. Young ladies of all genders. The coming community.

Do magazine penetrate target group?
Some mysteries are easy to penetrate.

A lot of pictures in magazine, no?
A girl accessorized with fountain pens. A big head of Pasolini. Girls like Dakota and Bianca. A man falling down in New York. Cheerleaders, monks. A Christian Dior ass. Snow. Shoes. New naked people. Termites.

A lot of text in magazine, no?
Daily compositions, schizophrenic business reports, people explaining things.

How old you?
30

How old magazine?
2

Where you live?
New York and Paris.

Address?
www.bernadettecorporation.com

You live alone?

This month with Seth, the City Indian.

You have partners?
Sean the designer in Providence.

You have favourite color?
Experts say black is back.

What is favourite color of magazine?
Black and white.

You like Colors?
No. Maybe color ads in Made in USA issue 4.

How edition magazine?
5000.

How real edition?
4000.

Why edition?
3000.

How much advertisements?
2000.

How much one page advertisement in magazine?
1000.

Who manager advertisement?
Bur Needet.

You good distribution?
It can't be stopped!

Distribution difficult, no?
Other people do the lifting and fly the planes.

You make profit?
Is life interesting in Holland?

How many?
A gay friend did a sex tour of Europe and said the biggest cocks were in Holland.

What is year income?
I couldn't find a salad in Holland to save my life. I was eating chicken nuggets on popsicle sticks. And drinking Chocomel. I didn't shit for 3 days. People were catching eels in the canal but not eating them.

What year income contributors?
I was at AVL-Ville in Rotterdam and they were playing reggae music and making toy guns. They said it was free state! There was no group sex like they advertise in brochure.

How design of magazine?
Steal boring pages from popular magazines. Subtract elements. Paste little shoes in the corners. Choose nice fonts. Vary densities. Let things fall apart. Find other ways out.

Why design?
John is handsome but like an unraveled thread. He carries a little box of tea tree oil impregnated toothpicks.

Who design?
Bernadette is a free spirit. She has been practicing wearing dresses. Cuts her own hair. Reads Kafka very slowly.

Name design?
Sean.

Address design?
Royal Academy of Nuts & Bolts. Providence, RI. skd@nine.org

Hour rate of design?
We reimburse his bus tickets and sometimes buy his lunch.

You have internet?
www.bernadettecorporation.com

Please teach me about the visual? Everything you get is right there in the middle.

Visual change, no?
One visual hides another.

You competition?
Everything,

You favourite magazine?
Tiqqun, Italian Vogue, RE.

Why favourite magazine?
Glamorous contagious retarded.

What is favourite magazine of designer?
Bop.

You are independent magazine?
No magazine is.

What is slogan of magazine?
Get Rid of Yourself!

I am so sorry for inconvenience but I have questions to write you for important interview. Please teach me some answers to questions?

Who are you?
I am Gert Jonkers. I am editor of magazine called Butt. I live in Amsterdam. Butt is sex magazine.

Why magazine?
Because Amsterdam is boring and all magazines are boring, not sexy.

Is magazine good?
Yes! Magazine *Butt* is wonderful and very sexy.

What target group magazine?
Cute boys.

Do magazine penetrate target group?
Yes but older women like it too.

What percentage?
Penetration for good magazine is low.

A lot of pictures in magazine, no?
Not too many, more text in magazine.

A lot of text in magazine, no?
Yes, lot of text, interviews! A lot of interviews.

How old you?
34

How old magazine?
Three months.

You have children, no?

What is favourite color of magazine?
Pink.

You like Colors?
No, don't like Benetton.

How edition magazine?
2000

How much advertisements?
11

How much one page advertisement in magazine?
$200

Who manager advertisement?
Pet@Name Models

Telephone number?
00. 31. 6. 24580191

Favourite food of advertisement manager?
That must be carrots.

You good distribution?
No, terrible distribution, please suggestions!

Distribution difficult, no?
Very difficult, nobody wants distribution.

You make profit?
Not yet.

How many?
Zero.

What is year income?
$40,000

What year income contributors?
Nothing

Hour rate of design?
Nothing.

Magazine made by Apple Mac?
Yes.

Who programs?
Nobody programs. At least not I know. I am editor.

Favourite program of designer?
The Antiques Roadshow.

You have internet?
Yes, I love internet.

How connection between Apple Mac and edition?
Yes, we have a website too: www.buttmagazine.com

How connection between edition and favourite food?
There no connection at all.

What is favourite food of partner?
Favourite food of boyfriend is sushi and boyfriend name is Rob.

Please teach me about the visual?
Always be clear.

Visual change, no?
Yes, I like long lenses now.

Visual important, yes?
Yes but good interview much important!

You competition?
Luckily not.

You favourite magazine?
Straight to Hell

I am so sorry for inconvenience but I have questions to write you for important interview. Please teach me some answers to questions?

Who are you?
I am Cory Reynolds, editor in chief of *Index*.

Why magazine?
Excitement.

Is magazine good?
Sweet, fun, sexy, good, dark, nice, friendly, sly, sharp, surprising and vivid.

What target group magazine?
Smart, curious.

Do magazine penetrate target group?
Deep.

What percentage?
Small numbers, large percentage.

A lot of pictures in magazine, no?
Yes, lots.

A lot of text in magazine, no?
Yes, long interviews!

How old you?
32

How old magazine?
5 ½

You have children, no?
No. I have a Portuguese Water Dog.

Address design?
Brooklyn.

Where you live?
Brooklyn.

You live alone?
No.

You have partners?
Jeremy Sigler. Fourteen years.

You have favourite color?
I like blue and yellow.

What is favourite color of magazine?
Blue.

How edition magazine?
Small, specific.

How much advertisements?
Lots of ads - from small Lower East Side and Nolita shops to big fashion.

How much one page advertisement in magazine?
Not too much!

Who manager advertisement?
Michael Bullock.

Magazine made by Apple Mac?
Yes. G-3 powerbook.

What is favourite food of partner?
Maryland steamed crabs.

Please teach me about the visual?
Index is warm, friendly, sensual, clean - but not too clean! We worked with incredible photographers, they like family: Wolfgang Tillmans, Juergen Teller, Leeta Harding, Brian Berman, Terry Richardson, Ryan McGinley, Patterson Beckwith, Roe Ethridge, Jessica Craig-Martin, Juliana Sohn, Matt Ducklo, Timothy Greenfield-Sanders.

Visual change, no?
Big changes. For the first three years, we printed black and white! For the last two years, we've go from half-color to full-color!

Visual important, yes?
Super important.

You favourite magazine?
The New Yorker, People.

Telephone number?
212.243.5981

Favourite food of advertisement manager?
Steak.

You good distribution?
Not so good. Distributors are like cavemen.

Distribution difficult, no?
Really terrible.

You make profit?
Almost.

Who design?
Stacy Wakefield.

Why favourite magazine?
Literary, fun.

You are independent magazine?
Yes.

How independent?
Entirely.

Why independent?
Very generous, totally committed publisher.

What is slogan of magazine?
We don't have slogan. I don't think we love slogans.

How your slogan?
Thanks.

You have Prada?
I have Prada shoes.

How design of magazine?
Design magazine good.

Why design?
Butt doesn't not not want too low profile. Without design no existence.

Who design?
Jop.

Name design?
Butt Design.

Address design?
Prinsengracht 397, 1016 HL Amsterdam

Why favourite magazine?
Because dirty stories in it, makes me come!

What is favourite magazine of designer?
View on Color, not!

You are independent magazine?
Yes, very much so.

How independent?
Totally, we are the boss.

What is slogan of magazine?
Fag Mag!

No, not want children.

How old children?
Always too young.

Where you live?
Amsterdam

Address?
Govert Flinckstraat 313, 1074 CB Amsterdam

You live alone?
No, with boyfriend.

You have partners?
Yes also.

You have favourite color?
Favourite color must be navy blue.

Myfanwy MacLeod

Moments in the Life of the Artist

The main thing was to stay focused and provide myself with realistic goals.

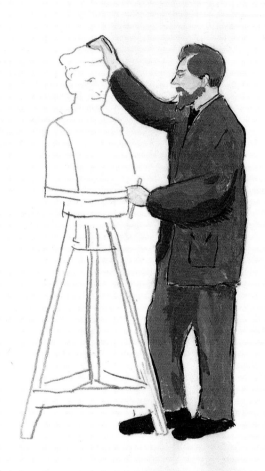

To spend your days in the company of naked men that was the
life for me.

Maybe I couldn't paint or sculpt, but I could work a mood better than anyone I knew.

True art was based on despair.

Colophon

Editors
Patrik Andersson
Judith Steedman

Design
Judith Steedman

Cover design
Thames & Hudson

Printing
Tien Wah Press

Photography
Floor Koomen
front cover
Carlos Mendes
documentation pages 31-33,
39-41, 77-79, 89-91
Judith Steedman
pages 12-17, 118-119, 229-233
and back cover
Patrik Andersson
pages 4-7, 18-19
Ian Skedd
pages 167-171
Linda Chinfin
pages 185-187

Special thanks to

Rudolf van Wezel
Willemijn de Jonge
Jeff Rian
Jop van Bennekom
Uscha Pohl
Roosje Klap
Floor Koomen
Yutaro Oka
Keiko Maeda
Maria Ben Saad
Stefania Malmsten
Tina Axelsson
Casey McKinney
Joseph Monteyne
Co Ito
Takaya Goto
Kaori Tanabe
Terence Koh
Myfanwy MacLeod
Ian Skedd
Robin Mitchell
Raif Adelberg
Brian Jungen
Greg Bellerby
Cate Rimmer
Kathy Slade
Elein Fleiss
Olivier Zahm
Winnie Terra
Liesbeth Fit
Jan Walaker
Kevin Hatt
Serge Becker
Astrid Stavro
Joana Ramos-Pinto
Dave Eggers
Miguel da Conceicao
Cory Reynolds
Bo Madestrand
Mike Simons
Cecilia Dean